Y0-BST-409

THE CHRIST OF THE POETS

The
CHRIST
of the Poets

by

EDWIN MIMS

GREENWOOD PRESS, PUBLISHERS
NEW YORK

THE CHRIST OF THE POETS

Copyright © 1948 by Stone & Pierce

Reprinted by permission
of Abingdon Press

First Greenwood Printing 1969
SBN 8371-2555-3

PRINTED IN UNITED STATES OF AMERICA

In memory of
My Mother

PREFACE

THE invitation to deliver the Shaffer lectures at North-western University—lectures sponsored by a foundation whose purpose is "to promote the appreciation of the life, character, teachings, and influence of Jesus"—furnished me the opportunity to relate this general theme to English and American poetry, to discover what the poets have had to say about this transcendent personality and momentous fact in history. The authorities of the university agreed with me that such an inquiry, or survey, would be especially valuable at this time when individuals and the world at large are so confused as to spiritual and religious values. Believing that poets have the gift of insight and imagination, that they know life, that they have the power of saying things in an adequate, felicitous, and final way, and that they thus combine truth and beauty in forms of lasting value, I am convinced that their answers to the question "What think ye of Christ?" or "Who do men say that I am?" are of real significance.

It is evident that so large a subject could not be adequately treated in five lectures. I have spent the intervening years since their delivery in 1944 in a more comprehensive survey of the whole field of English and American poetry with this central theme always in mind. The major poets called for a more intensive study, and the minor poets of the various periods must needs be incorporated as revealing significant points of view. It was especially important that I should consider more fully the many contemporary poets, some of whom have in quite recent years manifested an increasing interest in Christian faith.

I have found it necessary to leave out of consideration other fundamental articles in the Christian creed—such as God, immortality, morality, the sense of mystery, wonder, and beauty—that are characteristic of religion in its broad significance. I have omitted also a consideration of other forms of literature—such as drama, fiction, essays—all of which would be necessary if we were considering literature in its entirety. I have already dealt with these in *Great Writers as Interpreters of Religion*. Likewise, no account is taken of much of the poetry of the New Testament, which through the King James Version has become an integral part of the English tradition of great poetry; for it cannot be emphasized too strongly that many of the sayings of Jesus were poetic in their figurative language as well as in their form. For the same reason I have omitted any references to the great hymns which are the common possession of Christendom, whether we think of Gregorian chants, or the devotional verse of the seventeenth century, or the great volume of hymns that characterized the evangelical revival of the eighteenth century, or the more modern hymns of Newman, Tennyson, and Whittier.

For several reasons I am leaving out medieval poetry, rich as it is in many aspects of my subject. First, I am limited by space. And just as England has produced no Thomas Aquinas in theology, no Chartres cathedral, so it has produced none of the great medieval hymns and chants, and no great Christian poet like Dante. Even the poems that are of interest to students of English literature—such as those of Cynewulf, "The Pearl," *Piers the Plowman,* and a few religious lyrics and passages from Chaucer—have to be translated for the general reader; and none of them are good enough to win universal admiration. Another reason is that the supreme emphasis in medieval literature is on the Virgin rather than on her Son. Henry Adams, in his monumental book *Mont Saint-Michel and Chartres,* has made clear that the unity of art and philosophy in the twelfth and thirteenth centuries was in the worship of the Virgin Mary; in her personality is to be found the contrast with the greatest force in our modern world, the dynamo. Eileen Power, in her introduction to *Miracles of the Blessed Virgin Mary,* well says:

The cult of the Virgin is the most characteristic flower of medieval religion. . . . Everywhere the Virgin's relics were adored. . . . Great pilgrimages grew up to her shrines. . . . All the great doctors of the twelfth century, from the orthodox St. Bernard to the heretic Abélard, combined to honor her. Magnificent cathedrals were reared and decorated in her honor, and her lady chapel stood in every church. She could command all the best artists, and the poets from Dante downwards surpassed themselves in her praise.

I have tried to be catholic in my consideration of all possible interpretations of Jesus by including Roman Catholics as well as Protestants, unitarians as well as trinitarians, modern poets as well as traditional. Richard Crashaw, Gerard Manley Hopkins, Francis Thompson, to mention only a few of the Catholic poets, wrote with passionate intensity of their faith in Jesus as their Saviour. There have been many poets who have emphasized the humanity of Jesus in the same spirit with which John Erskine recently wrote *The Human Life of Jesus*, while others have expressed the point of view that only in his divinity can be understood his significance for the human race, a point of view fully elaborated by George Santayana in his *Idea of Christ in the Gospels*. I hope that the comprehensive survey of modern poetry, and even contemporary, may reinforce the testimony of those poets who may be said to belong to the great tradition.

In short I have adopted in essence the words of Howard S. Bliss in his poem "The Modern Missionary."

Does Christ save you from your sin?
Call Him Savior!

Does He free you from the slavery of your passions?
Call Him Redeemer!

Does He teach you as no one else has taught you?
Call Him Teacher!

Does He mould and master your life?
Call Him Master!

Does He shine upon the pathway that is dark to you?
Call Him Guide!

Does He reveal God to you?
Call Him the Son of God!

Does He reveal man?
Call Him the Son of Man!

Or, in following Him, are your lips silent in your inca-
    pacity to define Him, and His influence upon you?
Call Him by no name, but follow Him! [1]

Or to put it another way, I find in Richard Watson
Gilder's poem "The Song of a Heathen" an expression
that seems to coincide with the broad and catholic
spirit so often manifested by Jesus in his calling men
to service.

> If Jesus Christ is a man—
>   And only a man,—I say
> That of all mankind I cleave to him
>   And to him will I cleave alway.

[1] Copyright 1920, The Atlantic Monthly Co. Used by permission.

If Jesus Christ is a god—
And the only God,—I swear
I will follow him through heaven and hell,
The earth, the sea, and the air! [2]

My obligations to those who have treated the theme of this volume, either in broad outline or in special authors and periods, are acknowledged in quotations and citations. I am under special obligation to Professor Charles S. Braden of Northwestern University, through whom the invitation came to deliver the Shaffer lectures, and who has made many helpful suggestions. I am much indebted to my daughter, Ella Puryear Mims, for typing and editing the manuscript.

EDWIN MIMS

[2] From *The Poems of Richard Watson Gilder*. Used by permission Houghton Mifflin Co.

CONTENTS

CHAPTER I

Doubt and Faith:
A General Survey

FORTY years ago Canon C. W. Stubbs of Ely cathedral delivered a series of lectures at the University of Cambridge, which were published under the title *The Christ of English Poetry*. "It seems to me," he said, "that the Poets, rather than the Theologians, or the men of science, are the most representative of all writers on religious questions." He expressed the hope that through a quickened interest in the witness of the English poets to the personality of Christ and to the spirit of his religion there might be gained some consciousness, if only by glimpses, of his garment's hem. "The poets are the most prophetic, the most clear-sighted, the most deep-hearted men of their time." In the same spirit and with the same hope I have undertaken a more comprehensive survey. Dean Stubbs treated only some of the medieval poets, Shakespeare, Milton, and Browning. Even within these limits he did not always confine himself to the immediate subject, and he did not seem to be aware of other poets who illustrate over a longer stretch of time his general theme.

It must be admitted that the first impression of this survey of English and American poetry is disappointing and even disillusioning. It is very easy to exaggerate the Christian tradition. Canon Stubbs, for instance, gave a whole chapter of his volume to Shakespeare; but he did not, I believe, justify the inclusion of the dramatist. Aside from more or less conventional lines widely scattered, and aside from a passage in his will, there is no evidence that Shakespeare held to the Christian faith. One may come to the conclusion that his tragedies point the way to a faith in immortality, just as tragic life does; one may feel that such cannot be the end of man's suffering, but this conclusion is not expressed by the dramatist. "The rest is silence." One may think that Prospero, rising above all revenge in his forgiveness of those who tried to wreck his life, and master of all the forces of nature and humanity, is a parallel to Jesus himself; but here again the conclusion is that of the reader or the listener to the play rather than that of the author.

In the same way many individuals and groups of writers are not to be considered as having given expression to essential Christian faith. In only a few passages, such as the well-known characterization of the parson in the "Prologue" and "The Prioress's Tale," does Chaucer give evidence that he was a Catholic. What was said of Shakespeare is true also of the other dramatists of the Elizabethan age. The Cavalier poets— except Herrick, who wrote his *Noble Numbers* as a sort of apology for his "unbaptized rhymes," which are far more characteristic—give little evidence of the Anglican faith to which most of them were conventionally committed. Aside from a few passages Dryden and Pope might as well be called deists as Christians. Even Dr. Johnson, who was a steadfast conservative in his religion as in his politics and whose prayers as recorded by Boswell give evidence of real piety and devotion, left no poetry as an expression of his deep-rooted faith. The Romantic poets—with all "the renascence of wonder" that characterized their poetry, and with their deep sense of the infinite and the eternal, and with the undoubted belief in the Holy Spirit which inspired their loftiest utterances—left little that can be cited in this volume. It is well known that Wordsworth, for instance, was a consecrated Christian, but one would never think that Christ had lived if the evidence of his poetry should be cited. The only exception to this generalization with regard to the Romantic poets is Coleridge, who in his prose and in his conversations at Highgate was the forerunner of the Broad-Church movement of the Victorian age, and who in his "Religious Musings," written on Christmas Eve, 1794—several years before his most characteristic poems were written—wrote:

> Lovely was the death
> Of Him, whose life was love! Holy with power
> He on the thought-benighted sceptic beamed
> Manifest Godhead. . . .
>
> .   .   .   .
>
> From hope and firmer faith to perfect love
> Attracted and absorbed: and centred there
> God only to behold, and know, and feel.

. . . .

> . . . God all in all!
> We and our Father one!

Christian faith triumphed in the major poets of the
Victorian era, as will be seen in the chapters devoted to
them; but Browning and Tennyson were scarcely dead
before the inevitable reaction came, and we have the
"art for art's sake" movement represented by Swin-
burne and William Morris, the determinism of Thomas
Hardy, the naturalism of novelists as well as poets. In
other words, the way was prepared for the disillusion-
ment of contemporary poetry. The most widely read
poems that differed somewhat from the major trends of
modern poetry—*The Rubáiyát of Omar Khay-
yám, A Shropshire Lad,* and the poems of Rudyard
Kipling with their Old Testament rather than New Tes-
tament spirit—appealed to a wide public and to the
critics as well. William Butler Yeats, who began by
following the art for art's sake school of poets, rebelled
against the materialism and determinism of modern
science, wandered for a while in the field of Celtic
legend and mythology, and concluded by adopting both
the technique and the point of view of later poets. In
editing *The Oxford Book of Modern Verse* he said that
he could find few poets, and those minor ones, who were
at all interested in religion. In his own poem "The Sec-
ond Coming" he summed up the general intellectual
situation as he saw it.

Things fall apart; the centre cannot hold;
Mere anarchy is loosed upon the world,

. . . .

The best lack all conviction, while the worst
Are full of passionate intensity.[1]

He himself rebelled against the odor of blood that was characteristic of Christianity. He preferred the rose rather than the cross as the symbol of life. Ezra Pound lamented that Christ followed Dionysus and made way for "macerations." Housman, in his "Easter Hymn," contemplated the possibility that Jesus remained in the grave—"dead in vain," with no morning for the "son of man."

Among American poets Robert Frost, Edwin Arlington Robinson, and Robinson Jeffers wrote, in the main, as if no Christ had ever lived. A younger poet, John Peale Bishop, in his "Ode" wrote:

> There was One might have saved
> Me from these grave dissolute stones
> And parrot eyes. But He is dead,
> Christ is dead. And in a grave
> Dark as a sightless skull He lies
> And of His bones are charnels made.[2]

E. E. Cummings, the most radical experimenter with the forms of poetry, speaks of certain Cambridge ladies

[1] From *Collected Poems* (copyright 1933, The Macmillan Co.). Used by permission the publishers.

[2] From *Selected Poems*. Used by permission Charles Scribner's Sons.

who believe in Longfellow and Christ, "both dead." Langston Hughes, fretting under the injustice done his race by church leaders, exclaims, "Goodbye, Christ!" Philip Horton says in his life of Hart Crane: "In the late '20's and '30's to confess religious emotions in New York literary circles was far more damaging to whatever went by the name of 'poetic prestige' than the confession of any number of sexual or moral irregularities."

Many critics and scholars in the modern period have either ignored, or been indifferent to, or actually combated anything that savors of religious belief. I. A. Richards, one of the chief influences in contemporary education, says that the modern world is through with poetry in so far as it has to do with propaganda or philosophy or belief; and C. O. Matthieson, in defending T. S. Eliot's change from doubt and even pessimism to a strong religious faith, says that objection to religious poetry is a widely spread prejudice of today. The makers of anthologies sometimes seem to be united in a conspiracy of silence in that they omit so many poems which are distinctively Christian. Whether these editors are actually teaching literature or making textbooks for those who are teaching, they seem to ignore religious values. The popular *Oxford Book of Verse* and Untermeyer's widely used anthologies are frequently lacking in Christian poems that have as much poetic value as those selected. The editors seem to react from anything that savors of religious standards and values. Many of the anthologies of prose and poetry that are specially prepared for college orientation courses seem to want to relieve teachers of any embarrassment involved in the selection of Christian poems. Perhaps this may be due to fear of offending students or their parents by furnishing controversial material.

It is difficult to see, for instance, why some of John Donne's *Love Poems* should always be published and his *Divine Poems* ignored. They have the same qualities that belong to the metaphysical poetry which has been so extolled by contemporary poets and critics. In another chapter I shall show that the proper understanding of Donne's later career depends upon the series of poems he wrote after his conversion, and that there is a passionate intensity about these that lifts them to the highest levels of poetry. Why should there be so much emphasis on the distinct features of metaphysical poetry and so little on Donne's belief in the Incarnation and in the Atonement, which can be explained only by his belief that Jesus triumphed over sin and death, those twin realities which were like a nightmare in Donne's life?

Or, to cite another instance, why should the revival of interest in William Blake that has affected so many contemporary poets not take into account the fact that Blake was a Jesus-intoxicated man, as Spinoza is said to have been God-intoxicated. You cannot understand Blake without realizing the large place Jesus occupies, not only in his shorter poems that are among the glories of English lyrical poetry, but in his longer

and more involved and more obscure "Prophetic Books."
Why magnify the *Marriage of Heaven and Hell*, as Swin-
burne does so ecstatically, at the expense of the *Ever-
lasting Gospel*, or *Milton*, or *Jerusalem*? Blake himself
wrote in 1802 to Thomas Butts:

> Tho' I have been very unhappy, I am so no longer. I am
> again Emerged into the light of day; I still & shall to Eter-
> nity *Embrace Christianity and Adore him who is the Ex-
> press image of God.* . . . I have Conquer'd, and shall go on
> Conquering. Nothing can withstand the fury of my Course
> among the Stars of God & in the Abysses of the Accuser.
> My Enthusiasm is still what it was, only Enlarged and
> confirmed.

He refers to himself as a "soldier of Christ." All this will
be increasingly evident in the fuller discussion of
Blake which follows; what I emphasize now is the fact
that many of his critics and many scholars deliberately
ignore or combat what all his best commentators con-
sider the very pulse of the machine.

In many anthologies prepared for survey courses in
English literature increasing space is given to the poems
of Browning, but the editors invariably leave out most
or all of the poems that deal in a dramatic way with
the poet's faith in the Incarnation. Why are "Andrea
del Sarto" and "Fra Lippo Lippi" considered better
poems, as poems, than "Saul" or "Cleon" or "Karshish"?
It is foolish to say that poems which express the central
belief of Browning, as we know it from many sources,
are merely didactic.

A more recent illustration of the intolerance and even bigotry of scholars and critics is the reaction to T. S. Eliot's acceptance of the Anglican faith. Those who had hailed him as the greatest poet of modern times by reason of *The Waste Land*, "Gerontion," "The Hollow Men," and other poems that express the desolation and despair of the modern world now regard him as a lost leader because he wrote *Ash Wednesday, The Rock, Murder in the Cathedral*, and *The Four Quartets*. Edmund Wilson in *Axel's Castle*, objecting to Eliot's statement that civilization could not endure without religion and religion without a church, said:

You can hardly have an effective church without a cult of Christ as the son of God; and you cannot have such a cult without more willingness to accept the supernatural than most of us to-day are able to muster. We feel in contemporary writers like Eliot a desire to believe in religious revelation, a belief that it would be a good thing to believe, rather than a genuine belief. The faith of the modern convert seems to burn only with a low blue flame.

John Crowe Ransom in *The New Criticism*—and let it be remembered that Ransom was one of the first admirers and even disciples of Eliot—says: "The religionist in Eliot has gained on the critic as he has gained on the poet: in the distribution of energies. The poems have become more religious. The religious writings have almost displaced the critical essays." And then he adds: "Had Mr. Eliot only served his 'literature' with half the zeal he served his 'religion'!" It never seems to occur to Ransom that Eliot might have a maturer, a richer mind and a fuller heart by worshiping in a cathedral than wandering aimlessly through the desert.

An even later illustration is the attitude of a younger poet to a change in W. H. Auden. He laments the fact that Auden has gone from Freud to Paul, and has thereby forfeited his claim to be a leader of poets. The determinism and communism of his early days have been "transfigured by Christian optimism" and obedience to authority.[3] This outburst of petulant criticism was doubtless caused by "For the Time Being," written by Auden, who, it might be just as well concluded, has also come into a more mature mind and richer heart. Who knows?

So far we have been considering the unfavorable aspects of this survey. Let us now turn to the brighter side. How do some of the modern scholars and teachers who ignore, or consciously or unconsciously confute, the Christian faith compare with Francis J. Child, perhaps the greatest English scholar this country has produced, who in 1863 edited for the Federal soldiers an anthology entitled *Poems of Religious Comfort, Counsel and Aspiration*, in which there are selections from Donne, Herbert, Vaughan, Whittier, Tennyson, Mrs. Browning, and others, and which concludes with selections from the Bible and the Prayer Book. On the final page he wrote: "Blessed be God, even the Father

[3] Randall Jarrell in *The Partisan Review*, Fall, 1945.

of our Lord Jesus Christ, the Father of Mercies, and the God of all Comfort." One of the great teachers of English, who might have held a chair in any American university, was Caleb T. Winchester of Wesleyan. He was as fine a combination of culture and piety as any man of his generation. The spirit of his life is in the words he wrote for a hymn for college students:

> And let those learn, who here shall meet,
> . . . .
> To seek the God that faith hath found.

Many more might be cited who have not hesitated to interpret Christ and Christian ideals to students. A book by Professor Charles G. Osgood of Princeton, *Poetry as a Means of Grace,* is based on the ideas that the greatest works of art have sprung from religious exaltation and that "poetry may illustrate, reinforce, verify and illuminate Holy Writ." He contends that in times like these, if at any time, the religious implication should call for no apology, "since," he says, "I can discover in all criticism no ultimate sound theory which does not with all else take into account the basic human instinct for religion." With this point of view he writes of Dante, Spenser, and Milton, emphasizing always the spirit and authority of Jesus.

In other words, some critics and scholars emphasize the value of tradition. Whitehead has suggested the phrase "provincialism of time" as one of the characteristics of those who write from the standpoint of a contemporary period. I have already alluded to John Donne and William Blake as two poets of the past who have had much influence over contemporary poetry and criticism. Throughout this volume there will be many evidences of major and minor poets who find in Jesus an expression of this tradition of the English-speaking people. The whole metaphysical school, of which Donne was the leader, is characterized by a persistent and intense faith in Jesus as Saviour and Redeemer. The poems that appear in the anthologies scarcely suggest the wealth of the complete volumes from which they are taken. George Herbert, for instance, is known generally as the author of "Virtue," "The Gifts of God," and "The Collar;" but it is not realized that the whole volume of *The Temple* is permeated with the personality of Jesus—two thirds of the poems in this volume are intimate expressions of the relationship between the poet and the Saviour. Henry Vaughan is remembered as the author of "The Retreat," "The World," and "Peace," but not as the author of many poems in which nature is revealed and interpreted as the symbol of deep religious faith centering in Jesus. Richard Crashaw is known as the author of "Wishes for My Supposed Mistress" and "Hymn to Saint Theresa," but not as the author of poems that celebrate "the Name that is above every name"—poems which sprang from a passionate and very concrete realization of the presence of Christ as revealed in the incidents of his life and in the symbols of worship. Likewise Thomas

Traherne is the author of not only "Wonder" but many other poems in which the joy of life, the fullness of life, is expressed in the realization of the abundant life revealed in Jesus—a striking anticipation of the more radiant and dramatic poems of Browning.

If, as I have indicated, Shakespeare cannot be included in this survey, it is certain that Milton affords an abundance of illustrations of Jesus as paramount in his intellectual and emotional life. From the time he wrote "On the Morning of Christ's Nativity" and began a poem on the Passion to his old age, when he wrote *Paradise Lost* and *Paradise Regained,* he was always conscious of the personality and teachings of Jesus, although he was not orthodox in his views. A later chapter will develop at length his preoccupation with this abiding theme. It is not necessary at this point to do more than mention the even more striking Christian faith of Tennyson and Browning. All of which is to say, as does Alfred Noyes in *The Golden Book of Catholic Poetry,* that "the literature of our Western culture is not a series of disconnected explosions, but a living, growing tree, an organic development, with roots deep in the past, and a central trunk with branches, leaves and blossoms."

Even in contemporary poetry there is far more Christian faith than one would at first suspect. T. S. Eliot is the author of not only *The Waste Land* and other poems that reveal the disillusionment of the modern period, but also many critical essays and poems which suggest his progress toward a definite faith. That he at last adopted the Anglo-Catholic faith does not diminish the importance of his contention that religion is Christianity, and Christianity implies the conception of the church. It is his firm conviction that literary criticism should be completed by criticism from a definite ethical and theological standpoint. He laments the gradual secularization of literature during the past three hundred years, and this secularism cannot understand the meaning of the primacy of the supernatural over the natural life. He further contends that our spiritual faith should give us some guidance in temporal matters, that morality rests upon religious sanction and the social organization of the world rests upon moral sanction, that we can judge temporal values only in the light of eternal values, and that a Christian world order is the only one which ultimately will work. In his *After Strange Gods,* based on a series of lectures delivered at the University of Virginia, he expresses these points of view and deplores the decay of Protestantism, which he interprets as the abandonment of the idea of original sin and consequently of the conception of an intense moral struggle. He believes that the world is attempting to form a civilized but non-Christian mentality and that the experiment will fail. Accordingly he contends that poetry cannot be separated from something he would call belief.

It will not inevitably be orthodox Christian belief since Christianity will probably continue to modify itself, as in the past, into something that can be believed. It takes application and a kind of genius to believe anything, and to believe anything will probably become more and more difficult as time goes on.

These ideas are involved in his later poems, which will be treated in a subsequent chapter. The general spirit of these poems is indicated by a quotation from *The Rock*.

> And the Son of Man was not crucified once for all
> The blood of the Martyrs not shed once for all,
> The lives of the Saints not given once for all:
> But the Son of Man is crucified always
> And there shall be Martyrs and Saints.
> And if blood of Martyrs is to flow on the steps
> We must first build the steps;
> And if the Temple is to be cast down
> We must first build the Temple.[4]

The change in the point of view of Eliot is paralleled by that in Auden and his colleagues Stephen Spender and C. Day Lewis. Only one who had passed through a radical point of view and had come to a maturer one could have written such lines as the following by Lewis:

> Consider these, for we have condemned them;
> Leaders to no sure land, guides their bearings lost

[4] Used by permission Harcourt, Brace & Co., Inc.

Or in league with robbers have reversed the signposts,
Disrespectful to ancestors, irresponsible to heirs.
Born barren, a freak growth, root in rubble,
Fruitlessly blossoming, whose foliage suffocates,
Their sap is sluggage, they reject the sun.

. . . .

Getters not begetters; gainers not beginners;
Whiners, no winners; no triers, betrayers;
Who steer by no star, whose moon means nothing.
Daily denying, unable to dig.

. . . .

The break with the past, the major operation.[5]

In line with such changes in point of view one is con-
stantly meeting surprises where one would least expect
them. Swinburne wrote all sorts of pagan poems, agnos-
tic, deterministic, epicurean; but he also wrote "A
Christmas Carol" and "Christmas Antiphones," in which
occur such passages as these:

> Very light of light,
> Turn the wide world's night
> To thy perfect day.

> God whose feet made sweet
> Those wild ways they trod,

. . . .

> God whose heart hath part
> In all grief that is,

. . . .

[5] From "Consider These, for We Have Condemned." Used by per-
mission Random House, Inc.

Lord, what worth in earth
Drew thee down to die?

. . . .

Bid our peace increase,
Thou that madest morn;
Bid oppression cease;
Bid the night be peace;
Bid the day be born.

One of the biggest surprises in the Romantic period
was that Shelley, who in his younger days registered
at a Swiss hotel as an atheist and who in his later poetry
gave many evidences of the influence of Plato in his
conception of the spirit of the eternal, should have
written his "Essay on Christianity," in which he speaks
of Jesus as "the Being who has influenced in the most
memorable manner the opinions and the fortunes of
the human species." He asserts that the institutions of
the most civilized parts of the globe "derive their
authority from the sanction of his doctrines." Jesus was
an "extraordinary genius"; his profound wisdom and
the "comprehensive morality of his doctrine" have had
an incalculable effect on mankind. Rebelling against
the Jehovah of the Old Testament, the poet, as in many
of his poems, subscribes to the essential teachings of
Jesus, especially his conception of love as the basis for
the brotherhood of man.

In the greatest of his long poems, *Prometheus Un-
bound*, Shelley suggests a parallel between the suffer-

ings of Prometheus and of Christ. The chorus brings
to Prometheus a vision of Calvary:

> Drops of bloody agony flow
> From his white and quivering brow.
>
> . . . .
>
> See a disenchanted nation
> Springs like day from desolation;
> To Truth its state is dedicate,
> And Freedom leads it forth, her mate;
> A legioned band of linkèd brothers
> Whom Love calls children.

Panthea (Faith), who has watched with him through
the long night of torture, shows him a "youth with
patient looks nailed to a crucifix"; and the Fury, who
is sent by Jupiter to warn him of the fate such saviors
and redeemers must suffer, sees in the cross an emblem
of those who "endure deep wrongs for man" and thus
"heap thousandfold-torment on themselves" and man-
kind. Prometheus replies:

> Remit the anguish of that lighted stare;
> Close those wan lips; let that thorn-wounded brow
> Stream not with blood; . . .
> Fix, fix those tortured orbs in peace and death,
> So thy sick throes shake not that crucifix.
>
> . . . .
>
> Thy name I will not speak,
> It hath become a curse. I see, I see
> The wise, the mild, lofty, and the just,
> Whom thy slaves hate for being like to thee.

In his last poem, "Hellas," in which he forecasts a golden age for the world, Shelley writes:

> A power from the unknown God,
>   A Promethean conqueror came;
> Like a triumphal path he trod
>   The thorns of death and shame.
>
> . . . .
>
>   The moon of Mahomet
>   Arose, and it shall set:
> While blazoned . . .
>   The cross leads generations on.

Such passages justify Browning's contention that, if Shelley had lived longer, he would have become a Christian.

One might say a good deal about Walt Whitman as a poet expressing democracy and some of the essential Christian values, but one would scarcely expect to find in the midst of *Leaves of Grass* a poem entitled "To Him That Was Crucified."

> My spirit to yours dear brother,
> Do not mind because many sounding your name do not
>   understand you,
> I do not sound your name, but I understand you,
> I specify you with joy O my comrade to salute you, and
>   to salute those who are with you, before and since,
>   and those to come also,
> That we all labor together transmitting the same charge
>   and succession,
> We few equals indifferent of lands, indifferent of times,

We, enclosers of all continents, all castes, allowers of
  all theologies,
Compassionaters, perceivers, rapport of men,

. . . .

Yet we walk unheld, free, the whole earth over, jour-
  neying up and down till we make our ineffaceable
  mark upon time and the diverse eras,
Till we saturate time and eras, that the men and women
  of races, ages to come, may prove brethren and
  lovers as we are.

We should add to this a passage on Christ in his *Dem-
ocratic Vistas:* "[A figure] with bent head, brooding
love and peace, like a dove."

Equally unexpected was Robert Bridges' *Testament
of Beauty*—so different in poetic technique and in
philosophical interpretation from the poems of almost
classic form and beauty he had written during a long
career. His language and experiments in verse forms
showed the influence of his younger contemporaries,
but few of them would have closed the long poem in
which he had surveyed classic art and a wide range of
ideologies with a tribute to the personality and teach-
ings of Jesus. Classic philosophy had declared that
there can be no friendship between God and man be-
cause of their unlimited disparity.

From this dilemma of pagan thought, this poison
  of faith,
Man-soul made glad escape in the worship of Christ;
for his humanity in God's Personality,

and communion with him is the life of the soul.

. . . .

      . . . But the Wind of heav'n
bloweth where it listeth, and Christ yet walketh the earth,
and talketh still as with those two disciples once
on the road to Emmaus—where they walk and are sad;
whose vision of him then was his victory over death,
thatt resurrection which all his lovers should share,
who in loving him had learn'd the Ethick of happiness;
whereby they too should come where he was ascended
to reign over men's hearts in the Kingdom of God.

Christ has been ever since "the essence discern'd . . .
of all their human friendships."

This is the endearing bond whereby Christ's company
yet holdeth together on the truth of his promise
that he spake of his great pity and trust in man's love.
Lo, I am with you always ev'n to the end of the world.

. . . .

      . . . And God so loveth the world . . .
and in the fellowship of the friendship of Christ
God is seen as the very self-essence of love,
Creator and mover of all as activ Lover of all.

. . . .

      . . . God and man: but ONE ETERNAL
in the love of Beauty and in the selfhood of Love.[6]

Many instances of such flashes of insight, such sur-
prises, will be found in the chapter on contemporary
poetry—for instance, Edwin Arlington Robinson's

* Used by permission The Clarendon Press, Oxford.

"Calvary," Carl Sandburg's "Contemporary Bunk-shooter," but none quite as surprising as Ezra Pound's "Ballad of the Goodly Fere." Amid all the strange personalities found in all ages and in all countries and races by this singular genius there shines an interpretation of Christ by one of his disciples after the Master's death. The poem is a protest against the conventional idea of the mild and gentle Jesus, who figures so largely in popular imagination. If it were not so original in language and in form, it might be considered an echo of Blake's *The Everlasting Gospel*. It is a good illustration of how from unconventional sources and from poets quite out of the atmosphere of the sanctuary may come a revelation of another point of view.

> A master of men was the Goodly Fere,
>   A mate of the wind and sea.
> If they think they ha' slain our Goodly Fere
>   They are fools eternally.
>
> .   .   .   .
>
> They'll no' get him a' in a book I think
>   Though they write it cunningly;
> No mouse of the scrolls was the Goodly Fere
>   But aye loved the open sea.
>
> .   .   .   .
>
> A son of God was the Goodly Fere
>   That bade us his brothers be.
> I ha' seen him cow a thousand men.
>   I have seen him upon the tree.

He cried no cry when they drave the nails
    And the blood gushed hot and free,
The hounds of the crimson sky gave tongue
    But never a cry cried he.[7]

Not less surprising to those who had read the earlier poems of W. H. Auden—poems characterized by a revolutionary spirit and by a mocking ironic vein—was his Christmas oratorio entitled "For the Time Being," in which he reproduces the circumstances surrounding the birth of Jesus, the danger and fear of Herod, the homage of the shepherds and the wise men, the meditation of Simeon, the journey to Egypt. The general theme is that "the Infinite had to manifest itself in the finite and that the Word which was implicit in the beginning became immediately explicit." By the event of this birth the true importance of all other things is defined, and by the existence of this Child the proper value of all other existence is given. The chorus at the end of the oratorio sings:

He is the Way.
Follow Him through the Land of Unlikeness;
You will see rare beasts, and have unique adventures.

He is the Truth.
Seek Him in the Kingdom of Anxiety;
You will come to a great city that has expected your
    return for years.

[7] Used by permission New Directions.

He is the Life.
Love Him in the World of the Flesh;
And at your marriage all its occasions shall dance
   for joy.[8]

Here is the "affirming flame" for which he prayed in an earlier poem.

Two younger poets of the past decade suggest there may be a reaction against the mood of the twenties and thirties, a reaction we have already considered in Eliot and Auden. Robert Lowell won the Pulitzer Prize for the best volume of poetry published in 1946. Throughout his volume there are many references that show his vivid realization of the presence of Christ in the New England background he presents; also something of the ancestral tradition is there, though expressed in modern verse technique.

Delmore Schwartz has written, among many other types of poetry that suggest his radical ideas and radical technique, one of the most vivid pictures and interpretations of the Last Supper. He represents the apostles talking together after the Master departed, and their general impression is that life will always be different because of what Jesus was on that night and what he said. No matter what they do, he will look at it; no matter what they say in future years, he will measure it; whatever they think thereafter, they will think of this communion; no matter what place they go to, he

[8] Used by permission Random House, Inc.

will touch it; no matter what may be done by them or by men in other ages, he has anticipated it.

> So spoke the twelfth; and then the twelve in chorus:
> "Unspeakable unnatural goodness is
> Risen and shines, and never will ignore us;
> He glows forever in all consciousness;
> Forgiveness, love, and hope possess the pit,
>
> .   .   .   .
> No matter what we do, he stares at it!
>
> .   .   .   .
> We know he looks at us like all the stars,
> And we shall never be as once we were,
> This life will never be what once it was!" [9]

Such poems as these and many others may be of great service to preachers in the interpretation of the Master. It is very apparent that the leading preachers of America have been much disturbed over the situation that now exists in the world. One of the most challenging books of recent years is George A. Buttrick's *Christ and Man's Dilemma,* which grew out of another series of lectures delivered under the auspices of the Shaffer Foundation. The book was born out of the travail of his soul as he considered the significance of the atomic bomb and its probable effect on our modern civilization.

Hermann Hagedorn, who has for many years written graceful and rather conventional poems as well as some significant biographies, seemed to answer Buttrick's

---

* From "Starlight Like Intuition Pierced the Twelve." Used by permission New Directions.

book in a poem entitled *The Bomb That Fell on America*. The first part is a vivid account of what happened in New Mexico and in Hiroshima. He is concerned with what the bomb will mean to America, for he does not approve of its use.

> We have victory without assurance,
> Power without direction,
> Responsibility without devotion,
> Opportunity without vision.

He is profoundly concerned with the religious aspects of the question as to how we shall rise to the challenge of this hour. He appeals to God to show the world the way out of this terrible dilemma. The Lord is represented as speaking to him in the desert and showing him the vision of the Man on the Cross, and asking for the difference between that Man and all others.

> "What do you see?" said the Voice.
> "I have never been crucified," I said.
> "No," said the Voice, "you have never been crucified.
> Do you know why?"
> I felt suddenly ashamed. "I have never made people
>   angry enough."
>
> .   .   .   .
>
> "The world is sick," said the Voice, "for dearth of
>   crucifixions.
>
> .   .   .   .
>
> I tremble for a world that has no crucifixions."

I felt a chasm open, and stood on the edge and shrank
  back.
"Lord, let me go," I cried. "Let me go back to my world!"
"Not yet. Look again, look deep, and say what you see."
"I've talked about love, but I myself never loved."
"What else?"

.   .   .   .

"I've talked about truth but I never dared look in her
  face."
"Oh, why, man, why," cried the Lord, and I knew that
  He too was in agony, "why, why did you not dare?"

.   .   .   .

"The Man on the Cross," said the Voice, "was not timid."
I sank at the foot of the Cross.
"Truth is not in me. I have fed on lies."

With this revelation of deep meaning he flees across
the world with the voice of the Lord in his ears. He
feels that the end of the world has come, but the Voice
says:

This is the beginning, this is daybreak.
Give me your life, and day shall be like a new world.

.   .   .   .

God and man together, We are such power as not all
  the atoms in all Creation can match!

Out of this new revelation comes the climax of the
poem—a splendid vision of what America may be if
men release the energies of the soul as they have
released the energy of the atom. In one of the most

powerful appeals to teachers and preachers he concludes:

"THERE IS POWER IN THE HUMAN SOUL," SAID THE LORD,
"WHEN YOU BREAK THROUGH AND SET IT FREE.
LIKE THE POWER OF THE ATOM,
MORE POWERFUL THAN THE ATOM,
IT CAN CONTROL THE ATOM,
THE ONLY THING IN THE WORLD THAT CAN.
I TOLD YOU THAT THE ATOM IS THE GREATEST FORCE IN THE
WORLD, SAVE ONE.
THAT ONE IS THE HUMAN SOUL!" [10]

[10] Pacific Coast Publishing Co., Santa Barbara, Calif. Used by permission.

CHAPTER II

Edmund Spenser:
Platonist and Christian

LET us begin our survey with Edmund Spenser, who suggests much of the picturesqueness and atmosphere of the Middle Ages. Although he was allied in principle with the Protestants—even with the Calvinists, who dominated the early reformers and early founders of the Anglican church—he retained a feeling for Catholic imagery and tradition; and he combined with it Plato, who played such an important part in the blending of Greek wisdom and Christian faith. His object in writing *The Faerie Queen* was to portray the Christian gentleman, or, as he wrote to Sir Walter Raleigh, "to fashion a gentleman or noble person in vertuous and gentle discipline."

> A Gentle Knight was pricking on the plaine,
> Y cladd in mightie armes and silver shielde.
>
> . . . .
>
> But on his brest a bloudie Crosse he bore,
> The deare remembrance of his dying Lord.
> For whose sweete sake that glorious badge he wore,
> And dead as living ever him ador'd.
>
> . . . .
>
> Upon a great adventure he was bond.

The climax of his adventure was his vision of Holiness in Canto X (lines 483 ff.). After many struggles with evil forces he comes to the House of Holiness, where he passes through the processes of mystical contemplation —purgation, illumination, prayer—until he has a vision of the New Jerusalem, "wherein eternall peace and happinesse doth dwell."

> The new Jerusalem, that God has built
> For those to dwell in, that are chosen his,
> His chosen people purg'd from sinful guilt,
> With pretious blood, which cruelly was spilt
> On cursed tree, of that unspotted lambe,
> That for the sinnes of all the world was kilt.

The knight is hailed as St. George of England, but he must fight other foes before he can enter the sacred city, which he has seen in a moment of high vision.

That this faith in Jesus was not merely a part of the pattern of this great allegory is seen in Spenser's "Sonnet LXVIII" on Easter, one of the *Amoretti* sonnets addressed to his betrothed.

> This joyous day, deare Lord, with joy begin,
>   and grant that we for whom thou diddest dye,
> being with thy deare blood clene washt from sin,
>   may live for ever in felicity.

Such love the poet seeks in his own love.

> So let us love, deare love, lyke as we ought,
>   love is the lesson which the Lord us taught.

In 1596, three years later, he published the *Four Hymns,* made up of "Love," "Beauty," "Heavenly Love," and "Heavenly Beauty."[1] In the third of these he identifies Christ with heavenly love. The hero of the first hymn is Cupid; of the second, Venus; but in his last two hymns he gives expression to what has been called Christocentric and theocentric mysticism. The third hymn begins with an invocation to the God of love, high heaven's King. The poet apologizes for the "lewd layes" of his earlier poems and repents the follies of his youth as he approaches Heavenly Love. From the beginning God created in love. Then his eldest Son and Heir, "eternall, pure, and voide of sinfull blot," was crowned with equal honor, the "most lively image of [his] fathers face." Spenser calls upon the Holy Spirit to give him words equal to his thoughts. The angels carol hymns of love both day and night. When Lucifer rebelled, God sent him and his followers to hell and created man to take their place. The earth was made according to a heavenly pattern, and man was endowed with wisdom's riches. When he fell, Christ, out of the bosom of eternal bliss, descended in flesh's frail attire. As Adam committed his sin in the flesh, in the flesh it must be satisfied. "For mans deare sake he did a man become," though it meant he would be "nayled on a gallow tree" in order "to heale the sores of sinfull souls unsound."

[1] These four hymns have been edited by Lilian Winstanley, Cambridge University Press, 1930.

O blessed well of love, O floure of grace,
O glorious Morning-starre, O lampe of light,

. . . .

Meeke lambe of God . . .

The supreme question of the poem is how can man
requite Christ for all this good? He gave love, and we
must love him and our brethren. We must reproduce his
life in imagination—his nativity with the songs of the
shepherds and princes, his pains, his poverty, his
crucifixon. As we realize how he was reviled, scourged,
buffeted, we should "bleede in every vaine" and give
ourselves "unto him full and free" and "melt into teares,
and grone in grieved thought." Then shall ravished
souls be lifted to him, and bright, radiant eyes shall see
the Idea of his pure glory and be "kindled through
sight of those faire things above."

This summary can give only a glimpse of the music
and the thought of these stanzas. Professor Charles S.
Osgood of Princeton tells of their effect on one of his
graduate students, who said to him: "I am not what you
call a religious man. I don't understand those things.
But the poem had me converted. I don't mean the
argument. It was the music. Things that sound that way
must be true." He had in mind the whole poem, and
especially its conclusion:

Then shall thy ravisht soule inspired bee
With heavenly thoughts, farre above humane skil,
And thy bright radiant eyes shall plainely see

Th' Idea of his pure glorie, present still
Before thy face, that all thy spirits shall fill
With sweete enragement of celestiall love,
Kindled through sight of those faire things above.

Thus with the blending of the idealism of Plato
in the fourth hymn and the high religion of the Gospel
of John in the third, Spenser gives us an image of Christ
that parallels the mounting steps by which men, through
heavenly contemplation, attain the vision of eternal
beauty and love. The two hymns are almost exactly
parallel, especially if we regard Sapience of the fourth
hymn—"a Queene in royall robes"—as the heavenly
wisdom of the wisdom literature of the Old Testament,
or the Holy Spirit. Scholars have differed in interpre-
tation, some even suggesting that he meant the Virgin
Mary. "The faireness of her face no tongue can tell,"
just as no tongue can tell the glories of the Son.

Aubrey de Vere said of these two hymns: "Plato,
could he have returned to earth, would have found the
realization of his loftiest dream; St. Thomas Aquinas
would have discovered no fault; and St. Augustine
would have rejoiced." He might have added that the
author of the Fourth Gospel would have found in both
hymns a supreme expression of his own lines: "In the
beginning was the Word, and the Word was with God,
and the Word was God. . . . In him was life; and the
life was the light of men." This light shone in the mind
and heart of Edmund Spenser, and he comprehended
it.

47

CHAPTER III

John Donne:
Preacher and Poet

SPENSER was a union of divers elements, rather typical of the many-sided activity and thinking of the early years of the Age of Elizabeth. All things seemed possible to Bacon, who said with a certain audacity that was characteristic of the Renaissance, "I have taken all knowledge to be my province." The myriad-minded Shakespeare, gathering up into his personality all the currents of life and art and thought in those spacious times, might well have said, "I have taken all human nature to be my province." Elizabeth managed to keep the people united in a period of great national ardor and patriotism. Soon, however, England became divided into hostile camps.

Among those who were torn by the conflict—and at the same time perturbed by the new science that was unsettling the minds of men and by a new philosophy that took the form of cynicism and agnosticism—was John Donne, one of the most impressive personalities in the history of the English church and of English poetry. In the sheer magnitude of his mind and in the influence he had over his contemporaries and successors, he ranks with Dryden, Dr. Johnson, and Carlyle. Neglected a long time, he has recently become the object of increasing interest because largely from him came the metaphysical poetry that has had a great influence on poets like T. S. Eliot and his followers. In his combination of intellectual subtlety and passionate intensity, in his wide and varied experience as a courtier, as a student, as a preacher, and as a poet, he commands our attention. Well did Edmund Gosse in his *Life and Letters of John Donne* say that at forty years of age he was "the most brilliant and gifted mind in the kingdom," "the most illustrious and the most admired religious orator in England," and that "to hear him preach in St. Paul's Cathedral was to witness the most dramatic performance of his day."

Evidence of the profound impression made on his contemporaries is found in the eulogies written at his death by the most prominent men of his day. The often quoted words of Thomas Carew express the general point of view for a suitable epitaph:

> Here lies a king, that rul'd as he thought fit
> The universal monarchy of wit;
> Here lies two flamens, and both those the best;
> Apollo's first, at last the true God's priest.

These tributes are paralleled in our time by a symposium entitled *A Garland for John Donne,* edited by Theodore Spencer, who writes of his "fascinating and bewildering personality," his learned and complicated mind, and the vigorous excitement of his poetry. His popularity was greatly stimulated by Hemingway's quotation in *For Whom the Bell Tolls* and by Virginia Woolf's essay "Donne After Three Centuries" in her *Common Reader*, second series.

"We have only to read him," says Miss Woolf, "to submit to the sound of that passionate and penetrating voice, and his figure rises again across the waste of the years more erect, more imperious, more inscrutable than any of his time." Poets as different as Rupert Brooke, T. S. Eliot, and Walter de la Mare saluted him in almost extravagant words: "We are suddenly dazzled and enthralled by a sheer incandescence of thought and feeling." Of his versatility and variety of moods de la Mare says:

He can be as intolerably coarse as Swift, as enthusiastic as Shelley, as imaginative as Sir Thomas Browne, as nimble and insolent as Mercutio, as thought-ridden as Hamlet, as solemn as the *Dies Irae*, as paradoxical as a latter day moralist.[1]

How did such a man become a preacher, and why did he come to realize more and more that Jesus Christ was the solution of the problems that had so long disturbed his soul? Even a brief summary of his life will reveal how he might well have said, "I have taken all experience to be my province." He was eager to taste violently every thrill—physical, mental, and spiritual —life affords. Born of a Catholic family that inherited

---

[1] *Nineteenth Century*, 217 (1913): 372.

the martyrdom of Sir Thomas More, John Heywood, and some of his contemporary relatives, he knew what it was to have a faith that was being persecuted. Precocious in his knowledge obtained from both Oxford and Cambridge and from his own wide reading in scholastic theology and philosophy; associating with the young lawyers of Lincoln's Inn and with fashionable circles at the court, "a butterfly of the court, ostentatiously flitting from flower to flower"; familiar also with such men as gathered in the Mermaid Tavern around Ben Jonson; passing through all the sensual experiences of love and yet treating them with a certain objectivity and cynicism; embarking upon the romantic expedition of Essex to Cadiz and the Azores; secretary for four years of the Lord Keeper Sir Thomas Egerton and thus associating with the most prominent men in the kingdom; suffering the humiliation that came with a romantic marriage, which ended in a term of imprisonment and subsequent poverty and illness; writer of satires upon all phases of London life—Donne had sounded the depths and heights of contemporary life, and had explored the secrets of the senses and the subtleties of the mind. And yet at forty years of age he could speak of himself as "nothing." As Gosse says, "One of the most learned Englishmen in the land, he was not a lawyer; a profound theologian he was not in orders; with a throng of excellent relatives and friends, he performed no part at court."

Somehow he found no rest, no peace. His ambition

for higher position at court or in diplomatic service was thwarted; at times he was on the verge of poverty and was always haunted by fear of sickness and death. In a poem written about 1608 he described what he called the "Anatomie of the World," much of which sounds like some of Hamlet's soliloquies; and indeed he and Hamlet were about the same age and temperament. "Man contracted to an inch, who was a span." "Oh, what a trifle, and poore thing he is!" The world's whole frame is "quite out of joint." The new philosophy "calls all in doubt." The universe is all in pieces; all coherence is gone; and man is "rotten at the heart." The world's beauty is gone, its color, its proportion. Corruption is in man's brain and in his heart; the world is a "cinder," and the tears, sweat, and blood of man cannot mollify it, for nothing is worth our travail. In him were the conflicts and longings of a troubled soul, a subtle and fantastic mind.

The very restlessness of his life, due in part to his experience and to a "hydroptic and immoderate thirst for learning," finally led him to seek peace in religious faith. It was a slow process. He early broke away from his inherited Catholic faith because it seemed to him at that time opposed to the national idea and because he did not like the Jesuits or the Pope. He drifted into agnosticism, but from 1608 on he was very gradually led to adopt the Anglican faith and finally the Anglican ministry.

His marriage to Anne More ended his many adventures in love and brought a certain domestic peace that tranquilized his soul. His study of the church fathers, and especially his indictment of the Counter Reformation as contrasted with the Anglican church; the influence of the noble lady, Lady Magdalen Herbert, mother of the saintly George Herbert; his failure to receive any position worthy of his great talents; his consequent moods of depression; and finally the insistence of James I that he would make a great preacher —all these elements entered into his conversion and dedication. The death of his wife in 1617 produced in him a melancholy and a solitude that led eventually to his deeper faith. "Despair behind, death before" led him to faith hard won. One of his prayers is indicative of his struggle: "Thou hast set up many candlesticks and kindled many lamps in me, but I have either blown them out, or carried them to guide me in by-and-forbidden ways." His decision to be a minister was expressed in these words: "And so, blessed Jesus, I do take Thy cup of salvation, and will call upon Thy Name, and will preach Thy gospel." The dramatic needs of his whole being were now at last satisfied.

In a poem he wrote later to a young man who had just taken orders, he expressed his feeling about becoming a minister:

> Why doth the foolish world scorne that profession
> Whose joys pass speech? Why do they think unfit
> That gentry should join families with it?

As if their day were only to be spent
In dressing, mistressing and complement.

. . . .

What function is so noble as to be
Ambassador to God and destiny?
To open life? to give kingdoms to more
Than kings give dignities? to keep heaven's door?
Mary's prerogative was to bear Christ, so
'Tis preacher's to convey him, for they do,
As angels out of clouds, from pulpits speak,
And bless the poor beneath, the lame, the weak.

. . . .

How brave are those, who with their engine can
Bring man to heaven, and heaven again to man?

It does not fall within our survey to consider further
Donne as a preacher. His sermons have been the spe-
cial joy of many who were attracted to them not so
much by their theology or morality as by their literary
qualities. The selections from his sermons made by
Logan Pearsall Smith have attracted many readers.
Those who had never known anything of him as a
preacher or as a poet were recently drawn to him by the
quotation Hemingway used to strike the keynote of his
novel as well as to furnish his title. I quote the passage
because it emphasizes one of the dominant themes of
Donne's poems.

No man is an *Iland,* intire of it selfe; every man is a peece
of the Continent, a part of the *maine;* . . . any mans death
diminishes *me,* because I am involved in *Mankinde;* and

therefore never send to know for whom the *bell* tolls; It tolls for *thee*.

That bell was constantly sounding in Donne's ears. No man ever expressed in so many ways his fear of death; with his imagination he visualized every aspect of the decay and corruption of the body; aware of beauty as he was, he felt all the more keenly the loss of the earth and the corruption of the body. In his earlier love poetry, like most epicureans, he was conscious of death as the end of all—he contemplated someone finding his own body in a tomb with "a bracelet of bright hair about his bone." As T. S. Eliot says, "He knew the anguish of the marrow, the fever of the bone." He was enamored of death as a supernatural mistress who both fascinated and terrified him. Death was constantly with him in his home; he lost his patient wife and more than half his children. In his elegies and funeral sermons he lived every detail of death. His fascinated horror of death embittered his boast of eternal life. In the *Devotions,* written during and after a long illness, he gives every minute particular of the stages of sickness and the final recovery from what seemed like inevitable death. He might have said with Poe:

> The play is the tragedy, "Man,"
> And its Hero the Conqueror Worm.

In a dramatic gesture before his congregation he preached his final sermon on "the issues of death," stirring them deeply as he himself seemed to be passing out of life even while he spoke; and then in a still more dramatic gesture he dressed himself in a shroud and served as a model for the artist who wrought out this image as a permanent monument in St. Paul's when he should pass away.

I emphasize the horror of death because the central faith of Donne was that Christ had, by his death and resurrection, opened up to man the vision of triumph over death. Only at the last was Donne perfectly sure in this faith. In one of his sonnets written in 1618 he enacts "his play's last scene," his "pilgrimage's last mile." He pictures gluttonous death as unjointing his body and soul, but calls upon his Lord to save him from hell by imputing righteousness to him and thus purging him of evil. In another sonnet with a vigor of imagination that has rarely been surpassed he calls upon the angels to "blow their trumpets at the round earth's imagined corners," and thus to awaken the infinities of souls from their slumber in the earth. But he asks them to wait awhile, that he may once more repent of his sins and be sealed in pardon by the blood of Christ.

> Death, be not proud, though some have callèd thee
> Mighty and dreadful, for thou art not so:
> For those whom thou think'st thou dost overthrow
> Die not, poor Death; nor yet canst thou kill me.
> From Rest and Sleep, which but thy picture be,
> Much pleasure, then from thee much more must flow;
> And soonest our best men with thee do go—
> Rest of their bones and souls' delivery!

Thou'rt slave to fate, chance, kings, and desperate men,
And dost with poison, war, and sickness dwell;
And poppy or charms can make us sleep as well
And better than thy stroke. Why swell'st thou then?
One short sleep past, we wake eternally,
And Death shall be no more; Death, thou shalt die!

The other dominant note in Donne's sermons and poems is sin. Not even Bunyan conceived more vividly the facts and results of sin or sought more to be saved from sin. Donne's early passionate life and his knowledge of the world's dissipation lived constantly in his mind and heart. The struggle was never over, even to the very last. He called upon God to batter his heart until he yielded. His most frequently quoted poem, "A Hymne to God the Father," puts this idea of a never-ending struggle in passionate language.

I

Wilt thou forgive that sin where I begun,
   Which was my sin, though it were done before?
Wilt thou forgive that sin, through which I run
   And do run still, though still I do deplore?
When thou hast done, thou hast not done;
   For I have more.

II

Wilt thou forgive that sin, which I have won
   Others to sin, and made my sins their door?
Wilt thou forgive that sin, which I did shun
   A year or two, but wallowed in a score?
When thou hast done, thou hast not done;
   For I have more.

III

I have a sin of fear, that when I've spun
My last thread, I shall perish on the shore;
But swear by thyself, that at my death thy Son
Shall shine, as he shines now and heretofore:
And having done that, thou hast done;
I fear no more.

He said in one of his sermons that the blood of the Saviour ran in his veins.

Against this vermination, against this gnawing of the worme, that may bore through, and sink the strongest vessel that sails in the seas of the world, there is no other varnish, no other medicament, no other pitch nor rosin against this worme, but the blood of Christ Jesus.

The many references to sin in his sermons are paralleled in his "Litany":

From needing danger, to be good,
From owing thee yesterday's tears to-day,
From trusting so much to thy blood,
That in that hope we wound our souls away
From bribing thee with alms, t'excuse
Some sin more burdenous.

. . . .

From tempting Satan to tempt us . . .

He refers to a speechless sin, a whispering sin, which we hear only in our own consciousness; and beyond all these, original sin, which embraces all others, haunted his imagination—"that snake in my bosom, that poison in my blood."

Because sin and death were such realities in his experience and in his imagination, he was more and more dependent upon the Christian faith to sustain him in his struggle with both. That he finally triumphed over these two enemies of the soul cannot be questioned; nor can it be questioned that the central point in his faith—deeper than that in the church, or in the creed— was his belief that somehow Jesus had triumphed over sin and death and had thus made it possible for those who follow him to do so. No lust of intellect, no temptation to put reason above faith, no clear-eyed doubt could shake his faith. After so many storms at sea he came into the harbor.

Another evidence of Jesus as a central fact in Donne's view of religion is his views of the church. In an age of fierce controversies as to which was the right church, he maintained that all might agree on certain fundamentals—*real* fundamentals—and especially on the life and death and character of Jesus. As early as 1594 in one of his satires he criticizes those who turn to Rome or the Church of England or the Dissenters, and pleads for truth, which is like a hill whose summit can be reached only by careful circling or inquiry. Therefore we must "doubt wisely." He later studied more fully the controversy between the Romanists and the Protestants. "You know," he wrote to Sir Henry Goodyeare, "I never fettered nor imprisoned the word Religion—in seeing it in a Rome, or a Wittenburg [Luther], or a Geneva [Calvin]; they are all celestial beams of one Sun—i.e. Christ." He assailed the faults in all religions: "There are some things in which all religions agree: the worship of God, the holiness of life. . . . I will fast and pray as much as any Papist. . . . I will endeavor to be pure as any Puritan." He believed in one universal church, which "has but one ground, Christ Jesus, in which are rooted both the Romans and the reformers—branches alike sucking their vegetation from Christ."

In other words, Donne believed in the Incarnation as the central faith of Christendom. In one of his sermons he stated the doctrine in theological terms:

> The Lord, then, the Son of God, had a *Sitio* in heaven, as well as upon the Crosse; He thirsted after our salvation there, and in the midst of the fellowship of the Father and of the Holy Ghost. . . . He that was God *The Lord* became Christ, a man, and he that was *Christ* became *Jesus* . . . to save man all wayes, in all his parts. And to save all men, in all parts of the world. . . . To save this soule from hell, and to fill that capacity which it hath, and give it a capacity which it hath not.

More concisely and more concretely he expressed this doctrine in his poems:

> 'Twas much that man was made like God before,
> But, that God should be made like man, much more.

> This man, whom God did woo, and, loath t'attend
> Till man came up, did down to man descend.

God cloth'd himself in vile man's flesh that so
He might be weak enough to suffer woe.

It will thus be seen that Donne found expression for
all his religious beliefs in his poetry as well as in his
letters and sermons.

Some have drawn a sharp distinction between the
two periods of Donne's life, and between the two divi-
sions of his poems—*Songs and Sonnets,* written in his
early life, and *Divine Poems,* written after 1608. He
himself said that poetry was the mistress of his youth,
and divinity the wife of his later years. As we have al-
ready seen, his conversion was not a sudden one—first
his head and then his heart were committed to Chris-
tianity. But it is not fair to say with Edward Dowden
that, after he had taken holy orders, "he seldom threw
his passion into verse" and that "his ardour, his imagi-
nation, his delight in what is strange and wonderful—
all went into preaching." I rather agree with Sir Her-
bert C. Grierson, who is the authoritative editor and
critic of Donne's writings, that after the death of his
wife in 1617 there came into his sonnets and hymns "a
vigour and a profounder note," into his imagery "a
more magnificent quality," into his rhythm "a more
sonorous music."

In so far as his form and technique of verse are con-
cerned, there was no change. There is the same fusion
of thought and feeling—"unified sensibility," as T. S.
Eliot calls it—the same use of conceits, sometimes

strained and sometimes magnificent; the same colloquial language with a certain conversational tone; the same boldness and originality of expression, even to the point of experiments in verse. The poems of both periods are metaphysical in the technical meaning of the word. His muse was not converted. As Miss Woolf expressed it, the various lovers and countesses to whom he addressed his early poems were "replaced by a Prince still more virtuous and still more remote. To Him the prosperous, the important, the famous Dean of St. Paul's now turns, 'wholly sett on heavenly things.'"

One thing is certain: Jesus is the central theme of his later poems, and this theme rises to a climax in the eighteen *Holy Sonnets* written between 1618 and 1630. In 1608 he wrote a group of seven sonnets entitled *La Corona*, which included the "Annunciation," the "Nativity," the "Temple," the "Miracles," the "Resurrection," and the "Ascension." They were sent to his friend Lady Magdalen Herbert, with the hope that she would "harbour these hymns, to his dear name addrest," for they constituted a "crown of prayer and praise." The "Nativity" revealed "immensity, cloistered" in the womb of Mary, "miracles exceeding power of man," the one drop of blood that might moisten the dry soul of man, the hope of immortality based on the Resurrection and the Ascension.

In "The Litany," written in 1610 or later, he has echoes of the Catholic ritual but not of the Catholic dogma. The references to the sins from which he wishes to be delivered, especially those related to his own personal struggles, have already been cited.

In "The Crosse," which appeared in 1615, he represents the cross as seen throughout the universe. He plays with the idea in some of his worst puns and conceits. When he stretches out his arms, when he swims, he is the cross; when he sees the mast of a ship, or watches the flight of birds, or visualizes the crossing of parallels and meridians, he sees the cross. But fundamental is his conception of the Cross as a way of life and as the source of man's redemption.

> Since Christ embraced the Crosse itself, dare I,
> His image, the image of his Crosse deny?
> Would I have profit by the sacrifice,
> And dare the chosen altar to despise?
> It bore all other sins, but is it fit
> That it should bear the sin of scorning it?

"Good Friday" was written in the same vein.

Later than the *Holy Sonnets* are three poems which were written after Donne became dean of St. Paul's. The "Hymn of God the Father" is entitled "Hymn to Christ" in one of the manuscripts. In fact, Grierson prints the two side by side, the only difference being that in one "thy Sonne" is used, and in the other "thy Sunn." But whichever reading we adopt, there is clear indication that only the mercy of Christ can remove Donne's fear of death and sin. In the "Hymn to Christ,

at the Author's last going into Germany," he is opposed
to the seas which separate him from his parishioners
and to "the sea of blood," which is between his sins
and Christ.

> In what torn ship soever I embark,
> That ship shall be my emblem of thy Ark;
> What sea soever swallow me, that flood
> Shall be to me an emblem of thy blood.

Perhaps the last poem Donne wrote—for so thought
Izaak Walton in his incomparable life of the poet—
was the "Hymn to God, my God, in my Sickness,"
which parallels Sonnet XX, "What if this present were
the world's last night?" He is now coming to "that holy
room," where he will join the saints in music.

> I tune the instrument here at the door,
> And, what I must do then, think here before.

Through the straits of death he is passing into the sea
of eternity pictured as Jerusalem. For once he reaches
complete serenity above all fear of an angry God or
of death.

> So in his purple wrapped receive me, Lord,
> By these his thorns give me his other crown;
> And as to others' souls I preached thy word,
> Be this my text, my sermon to mine own,—
> *Therefore, that he may raise, the Lord throws down.*

CHAPTER IV

George Herbert:
Holy Shepherd

IN A sense Herbert was the spiritual son or successor of John Donne, who had long been a friend of Herbert's mother and had written two of his best sonnets about her. Donne had met the mother and young son at Cambridge in 1609; and in 1625, while the plague was raging in London, he had been a guest for several weeks in their home in Chelsea. It was at this time that Herbert was torn between the life of the court and the ministry of the church, and undoubtedly Donne had much to do with his final decision. Donne sent him a seal he had had made—the body of Christ upon the cross extended upon an anchor, the emblem of hope. It was an impressive way of saying that he had at last found peace and that the cross was his anchor—not a very happy conceit, however. The following year Herbert's mother died, and her funeral sermon was preached by Donne. Soon thereafter Herbert consecrated himself to the work of the ministry. To one of his friends who had contended that the ministry was "too mean an employment, and too much below his birth, and the excellent abilities and endowments of his mind," he replied:

It hath been formerly judged that the domestic servants of the King of Heaven should be of the noblest families on earth. And though the iniquity of the late times have made clergymen meanly valued, and the sacred name of priest contemptible; yet I will labour to make it honourable, by consecrating all my learning, and all my poor abilities to advance the glory of that God that gave them; knowing that I can never do too much for him, that hath done so much for me, as to make me a Christian. And I will labour to be like my Saviour, by making humility lovely in the eyes of all men, and by following the merciful and meek example of my dear Jesus.

Herbert had had no such violent struggle as Donne to come to this decision; he had no such "gnawing remorse and lacerating passion." When he was seventeen, he had written to his mother reproving the vanity of those "many love-poems that are daily writ and consecrated to Venus," and bewailed that so few were written that looked toward God and Heaven. Along with the letter he sent a poem, addressed to Jesus:

> Why are not sonnets made of thee? and layes
>   Upon thine altar burnt? Cannot thy love
> Heighten a spirit to sound out thy praise
>   As well as any she? Cannot thy Dove
> Outstrip their Cupid easilie in flight?
>   Or, since thy wayes are deep, and still the same,
>   Will not a verse runne smooth that bears thy name!

These words express a conflict that went on in his mind for several years, a conflict that indeed divides the poets and poems of the seventeenth century—"the unbaptized rhymes" of the court poets like Herrick, Carew, Suckling, and Lovelace, and the religious poems of the poets we are now considering. By all rights Herbert might have become associated with those of the court, for he inherited the traditions of noble families, the Pembrokes and the Herberts. His scholarship, and especially his knowledge of several foreign languages, distinguished him so at Cambridge that he became for several years the academic orator, making welcoming addresses to James I and Charles I and to other distinguished visitors. His patrons urged him to courtly positions. He was "handsome, graceful in person, elegant in manner, witty and gracious." There is no doubt that he delayed his decision to become a minister and that only the death of his two most eminent patrons and a naturally weak body turned him finally to the religious life. After serving two livings he was chosen, under the influence of Archbishop Laud, as the rector of Bemerton, a parish of only 150 communicants and a little church 45 feet by 18.

Think of the difference between St. Paul's cathedral and this small church as the backgrounds of Donne and Herbert. There was the same striking contrast between the two men—one dramatic, violent, intense, hurling his denunciations of sin and forebodings of death to his awe-struck listeners; the other gentle, humble, consecrated, a real pastor of his flock, a shepherd worthy of his Master. Helen C. White says in her authoritative volume *The Metaphysical Poets:*

> Donne can take us off our feet and for a moment carry us to a vantage point far above this world from which we can hear the angels blow their trumpets at earth's imagined corners. . . . It is along the roads of this earth that Herbert goes to meet that immortal Easter, and the dust and the chambers of his world, from which he wrings the secret peace of God.[1]

All who have read the incomparable short biography of Herbert by Izaak Walton in his *Lives* will recall the delicate art with which this devout layman pictured the life of the rural preacher, the country parson. Commenting on Herbert's love of music, his appreciation of the rituals and symbols of the church, and giving illustrations of his little nameless unremembered acts of kindness and of love, he closes with these words:

> Thus he lived, and thus he died, like a saint, unspotted of the world, full of alms-deeds, full of humility, and all the examples of a virtuous life; which I cannot conclude better, than with this borrowed observation:

> —All must to their cold graves:
> But the religious actions of the just
> Smell sweet in death, and blossom in the dust.

[1] Copyright 1936, The Macmillan Co. Used by permission the publishers.

A life so full of charity, humility, and all Christian virtues that it deserves the eloquence of Chrysostom to commend and declare it; a life, that if it were related by a pen like his, there would then be no need for this age to look back at the times past for the examples of primitive piety; for they might be all found in the life of George Herbert.

The volume of poems entitled *The Temple* is the precious lifeblood of this devout spirit. One can have no idea of it from the three or four poems—"Virtue," "The Pulley," "The Collar"—that are usually found in our anthologies. Herbert was not primarily an intellectual or a partisan in the fierce religious controversies of his age; there breathes throughout the volume the spirit of devotion, of piety, of simple faith. It is the one classic expression of the ritual and the spirit of the Anglican church in this, its golden age—comparable to the writings of Richard Hooker, Sir Thomas Browne, Bishop Andrews, and Izaak Walton in defining the Anglican faith. Herbert had no trouble adopting this church as his own, for it was to him the golden mean between the Roman Catholic church and the various branches of the Puritan church. He found in it the tradition of beauty "neither too mean, nor yet too gay," neither painted nor undressed, neither ornate nor too simple. The church had "the perfect lineaments" and "hue both sweet and bright."

Herbert is pre-eminently a poet of the Church; his similes are drawn from her ceremonial; his most solemn thoughts are born of her mysteries; his tenderest lessons are taught by her prayers.[2]

We have in *The Temple* descriptions of the Bemerton church—the porch, the altar, the windows, some of them with fourteenth-century glass—the calendar of the religious year, the ceremonies of baptism and Holy Communion; but the most striking fact is the presence of the Master in all these forms and ceremonies. All outward forms were means to an end. Of the 169 poems that make up the volume, fully one half suggest some aspect of the Saviour's life or some evidences of his actual presence. The book is dedicated to him, in whose service he "found perfect freedom."

Lord, my first fruits present themselves to thee;
  Yet mine neither: for from thee they came,
And must return. Accept of them and me,
  And make us strive, who shall sing best thy name.

In the poem entitled "The Odour," which is suggestive of the atmosphere and incense of a temple service, he writes:

How sweetly doth my Master sound! My Master!
  As Amber-greese leaves a rich scent
    Unto the taster:
  So do these words a sweet content,
An orientall fragrancie, My Master.

[2] Robert A. Willmott, *The Works of George Herbert.*

With these all day I do perfume my minde,
My mind ev'n thrust into them both;
That I might finde
What cordials make this curious broth,
This broth of smells, that feeds and fats my minde.

"Easter," a typical calendar poem, begins with an ex-
clamation, "Rise heart; thy Lord is risen," and ends:

I got me flowers to straw thy way;
I got me boughs off many a tree;
But thou wast up by break of day,
And broughtst thy sweets along with thee.

In "Peace" he is asking where peace dwells—in a
secret cave, in the rainbow, in the garden? No. "A
rev'rend good old man" answered by telling the story
of the Prince who dwelt at Salem, really the Christ.

Take of this grain, which in my garden grows,
And grows for you;
Make bread of it: and that repose,
And peace which ev'ry where
With so much earnestnesse you do pursue,
Is onely there.

Herbert turned away from the courtier's and the
scholar's life, but he was always aware of the fascina-
tion of the life he might have led. He was honest enough
to confess a certain worldly tendency that was counter
to the life of piety and sacrifice. In "Affliction" he sum-
marizes the appeals made to him by "natural delights,"

"a world of mirth," "days . . . straw'd with flow'rs and happinesses."

> Whereas my birth and spirit rather took
> The way that takes the town;
> Thou didst betray me to a lingring book,
> And wrap me in a gown.
> I was entangled in the world of strife,
> Before I had the power to change my life.

In "The Pearl" he says:

> I know the wayes of learning.
>
> . . . .
>
> I know the wayes of honour, what maintains
> The quick returns of courtesie and wit.
>
> . . . .
>
> I know the wayes of pleasure, the sweet strains,
> The lullings and the relishes of it;
>
> . . . .
>
> What mirth and musick mean.

But these cannot interfere with his love of his Lord.

> I know all these, and have them in my hand:
> Therefore not sealed, but with open eyes
> I flie to thee.
>
> . . . .
>
> But thy silk-twist let down from heav'n to me,
> Did both conduct and teach me, how by it
> To climb to thee.

In "The Quip" Beauty, Money, Glory, Wit, and Conversation make their claims on him, but he will let God answer for him.

> Yet when the houre of thy designe
>   To answer these fine things shall come;
> Speak not at large, say, I am thine,
>   And then they have their answer home.

Throughout the volume are poems in which Herbert talks directly to the Lord as if he were present in the temple. He is sometimes penitent, sometimes restless, sometimes seemingly cut off from consolation, and at other times rapturous in praise and thanksgiving. He sounds the depths and heights of personal religious emotions. In one poem, "The Sacrifice," he represents Jesus as speaking directly to him of his sufferings and disappointments in man, each stanza ending, "Was ever grief like mine?" One feels the tears in Herbert's eyes, the anguish in his heart, as every detail of the passion is wonderfully expressed.

> But now I die; now all is finished.
> My wo, mans weal: and now I bow my head:
> Onely let others say, when I am dead,
>   Never was grief like mine.

In one of the poems he calls on God to throw away his rod and wrath and approach him in the "gentle way."

Then let wrath remove;
Love will do the deed:
For with love
Stonie hearts will bleed.

But in "The Collar" he seeks the discipline that may overcome his running wild. The poem suggests the sins of the individual and of the age. He would for a moment abandon the "cold dispute of what is fit and not" and ignore the death's-head made by Puritans to scare people.

But as I rav'd and grew more fierce and wilde,
At every word,
Methought I heard one calling, Childe;
And I reply'd, My Lord.

A more hopeful note is struck in an experience growing out of his discovering a flower's root in wintertime.

Who would have thought my shrivel'd heart
Could have recover'd greennesse? It was gone
Quite under ground; as flowers depart
To see their mother-root, when they have blown.
. . . .

And now in age I bud again,
After so many deaths I live and write;
I once more smell the dew and rain
And relish versing: O my onely light,
It cannot be
That I am he,
On whom thy tempests fell all night.

These are thy wonders, Lord of love,
To make us see we are but flowers that glide
    Which when we once can finde and prove,
Thou hast a garden for us, where to bide.

How different is his approach to death from the spirit of fear which dominated John Donne! "Once an uncouth hideous thing," death since the Saviour's crucifixion has "grown fair and full of grace." At doomsday "all thy bones with beautie shall be clad."

    Therefore we can go die as sleep, and trust
        Half that we have
      Unto an honest faithfull grave;
    Making our pillows either down, or dust.

The volume ends as it began with an invocation to Jesus Christ:

        King of glorie, king of peace,
        With the one make warre to cease;
        With the other blesse thy sheep,
        Thee to love, in thee to sleep.

At the threshold of beautiful King's Chapel of Trinity College, Cambridge, stand the statues of Bacon and Newton; and part of a stained-glass window shows a scene at Bethany in the home of Mary and Martha with Herbert as one of the guests to greet the Lord. Surely if ever a man belonged in that company, it was he—the holy Herbert.

CHAPTER V

Henry Vaughan:
Mystic and Symbolist

HERBERT sent his collection of poems to Nicholas Ferrar to be published or not, as he saw fit. Ferrar was at the head of a small monastic community called Little Gidding, the only community of its type in England. It was a haunt of ancient peace in this stormy and tumultuous age. Herbert wrote a friend:

> Sir, I pray deliver this little book to my dear brother Ferrar, and tell him, he shall find in it a picture of the many spiritual conflicts that have passed betwixt God and my soul, before I could subject mine to the will of Jesus my Master: in whose service I have now found perfect freedom. Desire him to read it; and then, if he can think it may turn to the advantage of any dejected poor soul, let it be made public; if not, let him burn it; for I and it are less than the least of God's mercies.

Ferrar was quick to publish it, for, as he said, "There was in it the picture of a divine soul in every page; and that the whole book was such a harmony of holy passion, as would enrich the world with pleasure and piety."

His prophecy was quickly fulfilled, for, according to Walton, twenty thousand copies of *The Temple* were sold within a few years. Among the readers of the first edition was Henry Vaughan, at that time a young man about London who had not found himself. After studying at Oxford and frequenting certain social circles in London, seeing something of the same life that had attracted Donne, he was so moved by Herbert's poems that he went back to his native region of the Usk valley, where he spent the rest of his life as a practicing physician and as a poet. In the first edition of a volume of sacred poems entitled *Silex Scintillans,* which appeared in 1650, he refers to the status of literature in England and especially to the court poets with their obscene, vile fancies and "the sinful, lewd contents." He himself had temporarily come under their influence, when the poems of Herbert caused him to realize that poetry might be the handmaid of religion; he decided he would thenceforth contribute his talent to the church, under the protection and conduct of her glorious Head. His biographer, H. F. Lyte, says:

The high and holy claims of God, the infinite importance of eternity, the worthlessness of the world and the folly of living for it, the baseness of sin, and the consequences of indulging in it, all seem to have pressed heavily on his mind at this crisis, and to have filled him with great humility and seriousness. . . . Just at this time he became acquainted with the writings of George Herbert and derived from them so much of comfort and instruction, that he determined to make the life and compositions of that holy man his own future models.

One can see many illustrations of the influence of Herbert on Vaughan; indeed there are many parallels between the two volumes of poetry, *The Temple* and *Silex Scintillans*. Vaughan too dedicates his volume to "My most merciful, my most loving, and dearly loved Redeemer, the ever-blessed, the onely holy and just one, Jesus Christ, the Son of the living God, and the sacred Virgin Mary." He uses almost identical words in stating, " 'Twas thine first, and to Thee returns."

> My dear Redeemer, the world's light,
> And life too, and my heart's delight!
> For all thy mercies and thy truth,
> Shew'd to me in my sinful youth,
> For my sad failings and my wilde
> Murmurings at thee, when most milde;
> For all my secret faults, and each
> Frequent relapse and wilful breach,
> For all designs meant against thee,
> And ev'ry publish'd vanity,
> Which thou divinely hast forgiven,
> While thy blood wash'd me white as heaven;
> I nothing have to give to thee,
> But this thy own gift, given to me.
> Refuse it not; for now thy *Token*
> Can tell thee where a heart is broken.

There is this fundamental difference between Herbert and Vaughan: While Vaughan was a devout layman in the Anglican church and wrote beautifully of the ritual and ceremonies of the church, his most char-

acteristic poems find in nature the suggestions of God
and Christ that Herbert finds in the symbols of the
church. In the quiet valley in which he lived, he
watched the coming of the seasons, the flowers, the
birds, the gentle river, the stars, and found in them
symbols and mystical experiences. He re-created the
world as it was in Eden, and he found "bright shoots
of everlastingness" that linked him up with both the
innocence of childhood and the realm beyond the stars,
to which his imagination often fled. His three most fre-
quently quoted poems—"The Retreat," "Peace," and
"Friends Departed"—have been used to classify him as
a mystic. Without underrating the influence of Her-
metic philosophy, of which his brother was a professed
adherent, one must realize the significance of the great
emphasis he put upon the life, personality, and teach-
ings of Jesus; to this fact must be attributed the greatest
importance. While, as we have seen, Jesus was a con-
stant companion and an actual presence for Herbert in
his church, Vaughan was constantly aware of him as an
intimate companion amid the scenes of nature. We see
this in the great majority of his poems.

For instance, in "Regeneration" we have a vivid de-
scription of the springtime, "all the way primros'd."
Every bush wore a garland, and his eyes were fed, "but
all the Eare lay hush." A little fountain, a bank of
flowers, a rushing wind suggested the presence of the
Lord, to whom he said:

> ... On me one breath,
> And let me dye before my death.

In "Religion" he is walking in the groves and sees in each shade an angel talking with a man. He thinks of Jacob, Elias, Abraham—"O how familiar then was heaven!"—and wonders why there are no such heavenly visitants now, why all miracles must cease. The church has darkened the vision, but he calls upon Christ to heal the waters and to bring his flock once more to the springing rock.

> Look down, great Master of the feast; O shine,
> And turn once more our water into wine!

In "The Search" after spending the night in "a roving exstasie" he greets the "pilgrim-sunne." He has been reliving the life of the Saviour—following him everywhere, from Bethlehem to Calvary. Never did tree bear fruit like the cross, "balsam of souls," "the bodye's bliss." He suggests that Christ is to be found in nature rather than among men, but even then there is only an intimation of his glory in another world.

> Search well another world; who studies this,
> Travels in Clouds, seeks *Manna* where none is.

In the "Incarnation and Passion" he wonders why the Lord put on clouds instead of light and clothed the morning star with dust. How could God be enclosed within a cell and the Maker pent up in a grave?

Ah, my deare Lord! what couldst thou spye
  In this impure, rebellious clay,
That made thee thus resolve to dye
  For those that kill thee every day?

O what strange wonders could thee move
  To slight thy precious bloud and breath?
Sure it was *Love*, my Lord; for *Love*
  Is only stronger far than death!

In "Corruption," which is strikingly like "The Retreat," he pictures the innocence and wonder of childhood and wonders where Almighty Love can now be found. In "The Law and the Gospel" he draws a contrast between the terror or awe of Mt. Sinai and the joy or faith of Mt. Sion.

But now since we to Sion came,
And through thy bloud thy glory see,
With filial confidence we touch ev'n thee;
And where the other Mount, all clad in flame
  And threatening clouds, would not so much
    As 'bide the touch,
We climb up this, and have too all the way
    Thy hand our stay;
Nay thou tak'st ours, and, which full comfort brings,
Thy Dove too bears us on her sacred wings.

These are but a few of the many poems in the volume which strike the definite Christian note. Like Herbert he writes about the various days of the church calendar—

Easter, Christmas, New Year's Day, and so on. He exclaims ecstatically the hope Easter brings:

> Death and darkness, get you packing,
> Nothing now to thee is lacking.

There are also poems covering every detail of Christ's life, especially the Nativity, the Last Supper, and Ascension Day. Of the latter he writes as he retraces the last steps of his Master:

> I see him leading out his chosen train,
> All sad with tears, which like warm summer-rain
> In silent drops steal from their holy eyes,
> Fix'd lately on the cross, now on the skies.
> And now (eternal Jesus!) thou dost heave
> Thy blessed hand to bless, these thou dost leave.
>
> . . . .
>
> Come then thou faithful witness! come dear Lord
> Upon the clouds again to judge this world!

Always he finds in nature symbols of faith, as may be seen in "The Flower," "The Bird," and "The Bee." He follows in imagination the bee as it wanders through the world seeking "honey in woods, juleps in brooks." Likewise, the poet would find refreshment in spiritual forms. He calls upon Jesus to furnish this balm of Gilead:

> Go with me to the shade and cell,
> Where thy best servants once did dwell.
> There let me know thy will, and see

Exiled religion owned by thee;
For thou canst turn dark grots to halls,
And make hills blossome like the vales,
Decking their untilled heads with flowers,
And fresh delights for all sad hours;
Till from them, like a laden bee,
I may fly home and hive with thee.

In "The Night" he recalls the talk with Nicodemus, who at midnight speaks with the Son. The Lord's head is filled with dew, and "all his locks are wet with the clear drops of night." The poet prays that the Lord may visit him in the nighttime, knocking at his door.

There is in God (some say)
A deep, but dazzling darkness; as men here
Say it is late and dusky, because they
See not all clear;
O for that night! where I in him
Might live invisible and dim.

In one of his most widely read poems, "Peace," he pays his tribute to One born in a manger, his gracious Friend, who reigns in the realms of peace.

If thou canst get but thither,
There grows the flower of peace,
The rose that cannot wither,
Thy fortress and thy ease.
Leave then thy foolish ranges;
For none can thee secure,
But one, who never changes,
Thy God, thy life, thy cure.

CHAPTER VI

Richard Crashaw:

Sensuous Priest

ANOTHER reader of Herbert's *Temple* was Richard Crashaw, who, on sending it to a gentlewoman, said in a later poem:

> Divinest love lies in this book:
> Expecting fire from your eyes,
> To kindle this his sacrifice.
> When your hands untie these strings,
> Think you have an angel by th' wings.
> One that gladly will be nigh,
> To wait upon each morning sigh,
> To flutter in the balmy air,
> Of your well perfumed prayer.

The circumstances of the two poets' lives were quite different and led in turn to quite different conclusions. Crashaw's father was an ardent opponent of the Roman Catholics and had stocked his library with many books that played their part in the controversial wars which swept through England. The son, like a good many other sons, was attracted and influenced by the books in quite a contrary way. After going to school at the Charterhouse in London he went to Cambridge, where at Pembroke College and later at Peterhouse he fell

under the influence of the High-Church Anglican faith.
He was well educated in the classics and in Spanish and
Italian. At first he wrote secular poems, very much in
the style of the court lyric poets. The most notable of
these was "Wishes for His Supposed Mistress." He
early became resentful of Puritanism, which he re-
ferred to as "a sluttishness far from religion." He re-
sented the idea that to be a true Protestant one must
go as far as possible in hating the Pope and the articles
of the Catholic faith. He frequently visited the Little
Gidding community, which drew him more and more
to the observance of watching, fasting, praying in the
late hours of the night; and he was interested in the
artistic printing, the embroidery, and the music of the
community. He afterward wrote a description of the
house, the only monastic establishment in England.

Meantime at Cambridge the chapel at Peterhouse
and small St. Mary's church with its beautiful Gothic
windows appealed more and more to his artistic sense.
While he was not a regular minister, he was a catechist
who became familiar with and regularly interpreted
the extreme forms and ceremonies of the church. Sud-
denly in 1643 there descended upon him and his col-
leagues the fury of the Puritan commissioners. In a
trance of orison, with the rich notes of the organ pour-
ing upon him and the light of the antique windows
surrounding him, they found him. They desecrated his
shrines, even the remote chapel at Little Gidding, and
they removed him from his fellowship because he

would not sign the League and Covenant. Finding refuge for a while at Oxford, where Charles's court was in session and the Anglican faith still flourished, he later fled to the Continent, joining in Paris the Queen, who had long been devoted to the Catholic faith. With the zeal of a convert he addressed a poem to the Countess of Denbigh, sister of the Duke of Buckingham, urging her "to render herself without further delay into the Communion of the Catholick Church." Why should she stand trembling at the gate of bliss and dare not venture to open it? He prayed that the dart of love, the arrow of light, might not fall upon her in vain.

> 'Tis cowardise that keeps this feild
> And want of courage not to yeild.
> Yeild then, o yeild, that love may win
> The Fort at last, and let life in.

With a letter from the Queen to the Pope he found his way in 1647 to Rome, whose splendor and worldliness did not satisfy his lonely and ascetic life. Under the patronage of one of the cardinals he was assigned in 1649 to Loreto, around which centered some of the legends of the saints. The central building was the house in which the Virgin was said to have been born, which had been transported through the skies by angels in 1294, and in which were the original altar constructed by Peter and Luke and the statue of the Blessed Virgin that Francis Xavier had visited. There he found at last complete satisfaction and rest.

To minister all day in the rich incense; to touch the very raiment of Our Lady, stiff with pearls and rubies to the feet; to trim the golden lamps . . . ; to pass in and out between the golden cherubim and bronze seraphim; . . . to hear the noise and mutter of the officiating priest, . . . the shrill sweet voices of the acolytes singing all day long— this must have seemed the very end of life . . . to the mystical and sensuous Crashaw.[1]

It is probable that Crashaw would not have left the Anglican church but for the civil war which broke through England. It seemed to him that there was no escape from the fury of Puritanism except in the arms of the mother church. It is interesting to surmise what Donne and Herbert would have done if they had lived to witness the execution of Laud, the abolition of the episcopacy, the mutilation of shrines, and the general desecration of St. Paul's or Bemerton. We have seen that the layman Henry Vaughan escaped to the peace of his quiet valley. Many others, both Protestants and Catholics, somehow lived either on the Continent or in remote places in England, waiting for the storm to blow over. Readers of Shorthouse's *John Inglesant* will recall the many secret places in which the Jesuits carried on their propaganda and ministered to the spiritual needs of Catholics like the mother of John Donne, the residents of Little Gidding, and even the inhabitants of stately country mansions.

[1] Edmund Gosse, *Seventeenth Century Studies,* p. 185.

Crashaw is the one poet who gave expression to this submerged faith—Southwell was an earlier martyr—the one poet in England who expressed in characteristic verse the spirit and the martyrdom of the Counter Reformation. His *Steps to the Temple*, published just before his death in 1649, with a later edition in 1652, is characterized by his vivid realization of St. Theresa and Mary Magdalene, his homage to the Virgin, and his rich and sensuous representation of the Nativity, the Crucifixion, and the redemptive power of the Master. There is about his poetry a voluptuousness of language, a richness and sometimes folly of conceits, an atmosphere of incense, which represent the influence of the Spanish mystics. Austin Warren says:

The world of men's inner life at its mystical intensity; the world of devotion expressing itself through the sacraments and ceremonial and liturgy; a world which knows vision and rapture, tears and fire; . . . a rhetoric, brilliant, expressive and appropriate. . . . The light passes through colored and storied glass and flickers from high candles; it illuminates an altar of purple marble. . . . A high mass is in celebration. . . . The air is redolent of rich, sharp incense. High above the chancel the rood beam exhibits a bold relief of the Crucified Lord and His suffering Mother; and in the church below there is the dusky figure of one praying and adoring.[2]

In this survey we are not concerned with some of Crashaw's best poems—especially with the three relat-

[2] *Richard Crashaw, A Study in Baroque Sensibility*, p. 206.

ing to St. Theresa, whose biography had been published in 1613—nor with those antiphonic hymns written in imitation of medieval chants. But there is more attention to Jesus than a hasty generalization shows, or the medieval tradition would demand. Even in the St. Theresa poems the climactic thought is her devotion to the Heavenly Bridegroom. After recounting her contributions to the development of the Order of the Carmellites and after suggesting the great number of converts who came to the church through her, he imagines her as entering the courts of heaven and being welcomed by thousands of crowned souls who will be themselves her crown.

> Put on, He'll say, put on,
> My rosy Love, that thy rich zone,
> Sparkling with the sacred flames
> Of thousand souls, whose happy names
> Heaven keeps upon thy score: thy bright
> Life brought them first to kiss the light
> That kindled them to stars; and so
> Thou with the Lamb, thy Lord, shalt go.
> And, wheresoe'er He sets His white
> Steps, walk with Him those ways of light,
> Which who in death would live to see,
> Must learn in life to die like thee.

And at the conclusion of "The Flaming Heart," which on the whole is an inferior poem, he breaks forth in the most passionate expression he ever wrote of his own personal longing and faith. He is addressing St. Theresa.

By all thy dower of lights and fires;
By all the eagle in thee, all the dove;
By all thy lives and deaths of love;
By thy large draughts of intellectual day,
And by thy thirsts of love more large than they;
By all thy brim-fill'd bowls of fierce desire,
By thy last morning's draught of liquid fire;
By the full kingdom of that final kiss
That seiz'd thy parting soul, and seal'd thee his;
By all the Heav'n thou hast in him
(Fair sister of the seraphim!)
By all of him we have in thee;
Leave nothing of myself in me.
Let me so read thy life, that I
Unto all life of mine may die.

Likewise, his emotional, sensuous delight in sacraments and ritual now and then is matched by a complete surrender to faith and obedience. His motto was:

Live, Jesus, live, and let it be
My life to dye for love of thee.

The section of his poems entitled "Carmen Deo Nostro" is full of devotion "to the Name above every name." His hymns sung by the shepherds and the kings might be reproduced as a miracle play, so vivid and real is the conversation between the shepherds.

Welcome, all wonders in one sight!
Eternity shut in a span.
Summer in winter. Day in night.
Heaven in earth, and God in man.

Great little one! whose all-embracing birth
Lifts earth to heaven, stoops heav'n to earth.

The morning and evening hymns celebrate that blood
whose least drops

... Sovereign be
To wash my world of sins from me.

He wonders in "Charitas Nimia, or the Dear Bargain"
why the ruin of man should have cost Christ so much.
Love is too kind, and such sacrifice shows sorry mer-
chandise. Why should worms or the prospect of hell
move such love? "Why should a piece of peevish clay
plead shares in the Eternity ... ?" He wishes that he
might see and realize how dear a price has been paid
for him. The worship of the Mother and the Son is ex-
pressed in the peculiar dramatic poem beginning "And
is he gone, whom these armes held but now?" In this
poem one can understand the large part held in medieval
poetry by this relationship.

He's gone; not leaving with me, till he come,
One smile at home.

. . . .

Yet sure thou did'st lodge here; this womb of mine
Was once call'd thine.

. . . .

Oft have I wrapt thy slumbers in soft airs,
And strok'd thy cares.

. . . .

Dawn then to me, thou morn of mine own day,
And let heaven stay.

91

Would'st thou here still fix thy fair abode,
  My bosom God:
What hinders but my bosom still might be
  Thy heaven to Thee.

Undoubtedly Crashaw, of all these seventeenth century poets, visualizes best the human life of Jesus, throwing about it all the sensuous beauty that is characteristic of the Catholic approach as seen in the great artists. As Helen C. White well says: "It was this appreciation of divine love condescending and of human love yearning for intimacy that led Crashaw to dwell so tenderly on the least aspects of the human life of Christ." [3] His poems reproduce the tone and atmosphere of medieval hymns and religious ballads, "in which the life of Galilee is treated much like life in the next village, and Christ and his mother talk to each other very much as did the villagers themselves." This intense, intimate feeling is best seen in his "Song of Divine Love."

Lord, when the sense of Thy sweet grace
Sends up my soul to seek Thy face,
Thy blessèd eyes breed such desire,
I die in Love's delicious fire.

. . . .

Still live in me this loving strife
Of living death and dying life;
For while Thou sweetly slayest me
Dead to myself, I live in Thee.

[3] *The Metaphysical Poets*, p. 236 (copyright 1936, The Macmillan Co.). Used by permission the publishers.

CHAPTER VII

Thomas Traherne:
Poet of Felicity

WHENEVER I am inclined not to believe in miracles, I think of Thomas Traherne, writing his *Meditations* and *Poems of Felicity*—both of them filled with wonder and mystery and joy—during the Restoration period, when English literature was at the dawn of the age of prose and reason. A still greater wonder is that his manuscripts remained unpublished and unknown until 1896, when someone picked them up at a bookstall in London for a few pennies. When they were shown to Dr. Grosart, he at once attributed them to Henry Vaughan, so similar was the opening poem, "How Like an Angel I Came Down," to "The Retreat." In 1903 Bertram Dobell published the first edition of the poems with an introduction which began:

. . . Centuries had drawn their curtains around him, and he had died utterly, as it seemed, out of the minds and memories of men; but the long night of his obscurity is at length over, and his light henceforth, if I am not much mistaken, is destined to shine with undiminished lustre as long as England and the English tongue shall endure.

His confidence has been justified, for the number of Traherne's poems in recent anthologies has steadily increased. Many readers have had the joy of discovering this poet, so different from any we have been considering. The first impression is that he is the poet of the innocence and wonder of childhood, anticipating the poems of Blake and Wordsworth; but a closer reading of all his poems will convince anyone of his relation to the tradition we have been studying. So far as we know, he knew nothing of Donne or Herbert, Vaughan or Crashaw; indeed, he is different from them at every point, except in his emphasis upon Jesus, and that in a totally different way. In contrast with the tortured tension and the complex personality of Donne, the quiet and serene peace of Herbert, the brooding melancholy tempered by faith of Vaughan, Traherne is pre-eminently the poet of joy. If one ever wishes a commentary on the words of Jesus, "Except ye . . . become as little children, ye shall not enter the kingdom of heaven," or a parallel to Wordsworth's "Intimations of Immortality," he will find it in the poems of Traherne. In "The Third Century" of his *Centuries of Meditations* he describes the innocence and joy of his childhood.

1

. . . Certainly Adam in Paradise had not more sweet and curious apprehensions of the world, than I when I was a child.

2

All appeared new, and strange at first, inexpressibly rare and delightful and beautiful. . . . My knowledge was Divine.

I knew by intuition those things which since my Apostasy, I collected again by the highest reason. . . . All things were spotless and pure and glorious. . . . I knew not that there were any sins, or complaints or laws. . . . I saw all in the peace of Eden. . . . All Time was Eternity, and a perpetual Sabbath.

This is only the beginning of many pages of prose that are paralleled in such poems as "The Salutation," "Eden," "Innocence," "The Preparative," "The Rapture," and above all "How Like an Angel."

There is nothing here of original sin—no serpent's sting, no stain nor spot of guilt, no dross nor matter. The world's fair beauty set his soul on fire. Wisdom, goodness, and love shone resplendent. He was one of the once-born souls William James speaks of. He came later to see and to feel the chains of custom, "the dirty tricks of the world," the misery and suffering of men; he realized what the fall meant for others, but there is no evidence that he ever passed through any of the conflicts we have noted in other poets. He knew the story of the redemption brought to men by Christ—his triumph over sin and death—but even the Crucifixion brought to him no such terror as we have witnessed in other poets. He believed that he could recover the joy and innocence of childhood by the right interpretation of the Incarnation and the Passion. It struck him as a wonderful thing that God revealed himself in man and that his own soul was thus deified. He believed that God was not complete until he took on the form of mortality. The divine felicity found its supreme expression in the gratitude, thanksgiving, and praise of man, and this voluntary act of love is God's recompense. He thus finds life and joy in the thought that he is God's image; he even fancies he is God's Ganymede. The very fact that Christ suffered for him is the basis of joy and not of pain. His blood is man's balsam, bliss, joy, wine. In his series of poems entitled *Thoughts* he expresses the joy and the blessedness of the highest contemplation, the joy of elevated thought.

> We drink our fill, and take their Beauty in,
> While Jesus Blood refines the Soul from Sin.
> His grievous Cross is a Supreme Delight,
> And of all Heavenly ones the greatest Sight.
> His throne is neer, tis just before our face,
> And all Eternitie his Dwelling place.
> His Dwelling place is full of Joys and Pleasures,
> His Throne a fountain of Eternal Treasures.
>
> .   .   .   .
>
> It enters in, and doth a Temple find,
> Or make a Living one within the Mind.
>
> .   .   .   .
>
> O give me Grace to see thy face, and be
> A constant Mirror of Eternitie.
> Let my pure Soul, transformed to a Thought,
> Attend upon thy Throne, and as it ought
> Spend all its Time in feeding on thy Lov,
> And never from thy Sacred presence mov.

He is not dependent for his joy on any material things, for he finds poverty does not exist when his mind is enriched with the things of the spirit. In the Bible, and especially in the New Testament, he finds that he is God's image and that men on earth are kings —"though clothed with mortal skin men may have angels' wings." Even London in its dazzling luster may become the New Jerusalem. On Christmas Day he hears the bells ringing from shire to shire in love of the King. How different were the bells that Donne heard suggesting always death!

In churches Traherne feels sacred joy, sacred mirth, as he realizes the presence of the Lord in the choir and in the holy hymns. The magnificence of cathedrals is like the magnificence of God. He wishes that there might be one church to which popes, kings, and rich merchants might come, as well as the humble people. He realizes something of the Mount of Transfiguration as he walks with angels and converses with God.

But all of this joy comes from the life and vicarious suffering of Christ.

> In Salem dwelt a Glorious King,
> Raisd from a Shepherds lowly State,
> That did his Praises like an Angel Sing
> Who did the World Create.

Jesus in the fullness of life became also a champion of chivalry, a poet, a musician, a lover of nature, a prophet, a judge, a sage, a philosopher. He encompassed all life and all truth and all beauty.

Perhaps Traherne's most daring thought is that Jesus broke down the bounds between soul and body. Each of the senses may become an inlet for the spirit to reveal itself, each limb a spring of joy, and every member crowned with glory. The fact that Jesus took on the flesh and endowed it with "the glorious excellence of God-head" caused the body to shine in the strength and height of all the spirit's endowment. The body is the temple of the deity. In reviewing the six days of creation Traherne describes the beauteous form of man, created with divine art:

> A rushing breath from heaven came
> Which kindled presently the vital flame.

Though man fell from this high state, Jesus enables us to see the recovery of man's highest faculties.

We are told that Traherne while a student at Oxford found all his studies a means of spiritual growth. No other man before Browning ever expressed so rapturously the possibilities of the total man, and the secret of his faith in such possibilities was his conception of Christ as combining in himself all the emotions, intellect, imagination, and creative will that may be approximated by those who follow him.

As Helen C. White in *The Metaphysical Poets* says:

He discovered that in the fact of the Redemption God had glorified him even more than he had thought possible. . . . That fact [Christ's sacrifice and suffering] which had filled a Donne with awe, which had moved a Herbert or a Crashaw to an ecstasy of pity and gratitude, which had focussed the more diffused feeling of a Vaughan into a deeper sense of mystery, meant something entirely different for Traherne. After a number of scattered but often highly realistic suggestions of the sufferings of Christ, he is moved to exclaim with wonder at the glory which must be the portion of the creature for whom his Maker would undertake such sufferings.

He that spared not His own Son but gave Him up for us all, how shall He not wish him also freely to give us all things? Is he not an object of infinite Love for whom our Saviour died? Shall not all things in Heaven and Earth serve him in splendour and glory, for whom the Son of God came down to minister in agonies and sufferings? [1]

[1] Pp. 344 ff. Copyright 1936. The Macmillan Co. Used by permission the publishers.

CHAPTER VIII

John Milton:
Dissenter and Heretic

ONE of the fancies I like to indulge in is imaginary conversations or debates or controversial pamphlets between John Donne and John Milton, the two most powerful personalities among men of letters of the seventeenth century. Milton was only twenty-three when Donne died, and his mind was still in a formative stage; but my fancy allows me to keep Donne alive till mid-century, when the religious conflict, accompanied by civil war, was in full swing. We have seen how Donne was led to accept the Christian faith and to become a Christian minister because of his increasing conception of the Church of England as the *via media* in the conflict between the Counter-Reformation and the extreme forms of dissent and nonconformity the Reformation produced. Milton would have attacked Donne as one of the chief representatives of the English clergy, whom he denounced in "Lycidas" and later in his pamphlets on church government; he would not have failed to comment on Donne's early sins and his close connection with James I and Charles I, his association with the court and distinguished noblemen, or his somewhat tolerant attitude toward Roman Catholics. Through men like Donne, Milton would have said vigorously and roughly and sometimes coarsely, England was being led back into the Catholic fold. Milton, on the other hand, beginning as a liberal Anglican, grew away from the church on account of its episcopacy and its alliance with the court and monarchy, then adopted the faith of the Presbyterians until they substituted "presbyter" for priest and tyranny for tyranny, and finally came to believe in a church free from forms and unrelated to the state, until he set up what cynics have called "the church of John Milton," himself the priest face to face with the holy of holies and owning no allegiance except to God himself.

There would have been a still further difference between Donne and Milton. As we have seen, Donne had gradually come to his conviction that the death and resurrection of Jesus furnished the only antidote to the sin and death which haunted his imagination and caused him to tremble and fear until the very last. He felt the need of a personal Saviour. There is no evidence that Milton ever passed through any conflict such as we have found characteristic of Donne and his successors. He had been from his childhood singularly free from any semblance of immorality, a veritable Christian knight, chaste as the lady in *Comus*. He had no sins to confess, no doubts to worry him, no fear of eternal punishment, no sense of alienation from God. He lived as ever in his great Taskmaster's eye and throughout his life felt himself under the guidance and protection of the Almighty. He was supremely confident of himself, even proud; he had been set aside, consecrated to a divine mission. His consciousness of God was the central note in his life, and not less fixed was his conception of the Holy Spirit, whom he invoked in many passages of his prose and in the more personal passages of *Paradise Lost*. What need had he for the Atonement? However much he may have accepted the creed as to the place of Christ in the general salvation of the world, he himself, unlike Donne and his followers, passed through no struggles, no temptations that called for a Saviour, a Redeemer.

George Herbert would have rejoiced in Milton's picture of

> Storied windows richly dight,
> Casting a dim religious light.

He would have found in *Comus* a vivid illustration or picture of what he himself had written in his best-known poem, "Virtue," but he would have shrunk in horror when he read that Milton said if Christ could be born in a stable, Christians might worship in a barn, and he would have felt as a personal affront the severe indictment of the English clergy in "Lycidas." There is no such sense of personal religion and devotion as we find in Herbert. Milton in his early poems, written in the beautiful countryside, reflected his feeling for nature, but he had nothing of the feeling for nature as a sacrament, nature as suggesting incidents in the life of the Master, that Vaughan had. Nor did he have any of the mystical joy Traherne associated with childhood and with the Incarnation and the Passion.

In fact Milton was a heretic from the standpoint of both the Roman and the Anglican faiths, and he went far beyond the dissenters, the Puritans, in the independence of his judgment, in the employment of his reason in all matters of religious faith, in his magnification of the free will of man. We shall see that he was an Arian rather than a trinitarian, that he rejected the ideas of predestination and election. He combined with his Christian faith the humanism that was characteristic of the Renaissance. Bunyan, Cromwell, and William Penn would have little understood his reverence for Plato, his feeling for Greek tragedy, his tributes to Greek philosophy in *Paradise Regained*. In fact in that century he stands alone, even though there are references in his writings to every phase of the life and thought of the century.

The question inevitably arises as to whether Milton can be considered a Christian. Lord David Cecil in his *Oxford Book of Christian Verse* says:

Milton . . . was not essentially a religious poet. He was a philosopher rather than a devotee. His imagination was lucid and concrete, unlit by heavenly gleams; theology to him was a superior branch of political science, the rule of reason and the moral law as exhibited in the working of the cosmos. Nor was his moral sensibility a Christian one. The Stoic virtues, fortitude, temperance, above all, moral independence, were what he valued. He did not live by faith, scorned hope, and was indisposed to charity; while pride, so far from being the vice which Christianity considers it, was to Milton the mark of a superior nature. As an exponent of the Christian spirit he cannot compare with Donne or Herbert. . . . As an exposition of Christian belief *Paradise Lost* and *Paradise Regained* are failures.

This is a very strong statement and, as I hope to show, a greatly exaggerated one. Jesus has a far more important place in his writings than this statement suggests. Cecil admits that Milton "is the greatest of English poets who have made religion their subject." The fact is that Milton's first poem of any importance, written when he was twenty-one years old, was "On the Morning of Christ's Nativity," of which he wrote to a friend:

I am singing the King of Heaven, bringer of peace, and the fortunate days promised by the Holy Ghost; the wanderings of God, and the stabling under a poor roof of Him who rules with his father the realms above; the star that led the wizards, the hymning of angels in the air, and the gods flying to their endangered fanes. This poem I made as a birthday gift to Christ; the first light of Christmas dawn brought me the theme.

This is an exact summary of the poem, but it gives little idea of the beauty of the language or the melody of the verse. It reminds one of the best of the medieval hymns. As Hilaire Belloc, himself a Catholic, said, "It might have been written by a Catholic," so sensuous is it in its beauty, so vivid in its imagery.

A year later Milton started a poem called "The Passion," tuning his song to sorrow and setting his heart to notes of saddest woe; but he found himself unable to proceed beyond eight stanzas and wrote: "This Subject the Author finding to be above the years he had when he wrote it, and nothing satisfied with what was begun, left it unfinished."

There is no reference to Jesus in any of the other poems of the first period of his career, nor in any of the sonnets written during the Civil War; but in his prose works he constantly cites the words of Jesus as the supreme authority on the many questions he discussed. In the definitive Columbia edition of all his writings, the references to Jesus fill forty pages of the index, showing that Milton had at his command every word Jesus ever uttered. In his *Areopagitica*—his plea for the unlimited freedom of the human mind—he makes a happy identification of truth with Jesus.

Truth indeed came once into the world with her divine Master, and was a perfect shape most glorious to look on: but when he ascended, and his Apostles after him were laid asleep, then strait arose a wicked race of deceivers, who . . . took the virgin Truth, hewed her lovely form into a thousand pieces, and scatter'd them to the four winds. From that time ever since, the sad friends of Truth, such as durst appear, imitating the careful search that Isis made for the mangl'd body of Osiris, went up and down gathering up limb by limb still as they could find them. We have not yet found them all, Lords and Commons, nor ever shall doe, till her Masters second comming; he shall bring together ever joynt and member, and shall mould them into an immortall feature of loveliness and perfection.

Lamenting the efforts of even Protestant sects to censor truth, he appeals for the utmost liberty in discovering new fragments of truth. Changing the figure, he writes of the building of the Temple of Truth and calls attention to the different works that men of various opinions and capacities may do in furnishing material for the structure.

As if, while the Temple of the Lord was building, some cutting, some squaring the marble, others hewing the cedars, there should be a sort of irrationall men who could not consider there must be many schisms and many dissections made in the quarry and in the timber, ere the house of God can be built. . . . The perfection consists in this, that out of many moderate varieties and brotherly dissimilitudes that are not vastly disproportionall arises the goodly and the graceful symmetry that commends the whole pile and structure. . . . Now the time seems come, wherein Moses the great Prophet may sit in heav'n rejoycing to see that memorable and glorious wish of his fulfill'd, when not only our sev'nty Elders, but all the Lords people are become Prophets.

It was a church of the prophets interpreted in this sense that Milton was visualizing when he called upon Christ to become the head of the Church, ready to lead the embattled hosts of Christendom.

Come forth out of thy royal chambers, O Prince of all the
kings of the earth, put on the visible robes of thy imperial
majesty, take up that unlimited scepter which the Al-
mighty father hath bequeathed thee; for now the voice of
thy Bride calls thee, and all creatures sigh to be renewed.

It is this Christ that goes forth in the sixth book of
Paradise Lost to overcome the hosts of Satan and to re-
veal the majesty and power of God. It does not fall
within the scope of this survey to treat Milton's great
poem in its many aspects. The majesty of its verse with
its organ-like roll of melody and harmony, the back-
ground of infinite space and eternity through which
the characters move, the presentation and explanation
of the origin of evil embodied in the towering per-
sonality of Satan and his associates, the revelation of
the perfect beauty of the Garden of Eden, the visualiza-
tion of a Utopia of innocence and joy when Adam and
Eve were fresh from the hands of the Creator, the story
as a whole which, with few exceptions, moves so fluent-
ly and grandly—all these I must pass over and con-
centrate upon the visualization and realization of Christ
as the only begotten Son of God, acclaimed as such by
the heavenly hosts on the day of his coronation, as the
leader of angelic forces against the forces of Satan, as
the creator of the world, and as the reconciler, the
Saviour and Redeemer, the final victor over Satan in
this world, as well as in the empyrean. It must be ad-
mitted that Milton has not succeeded as well, from

an artistic standpoint, in the representation of Christ as he has in the representation of Satan, but from the standpoint of the story itself Christ and not Satan is the hero; he plays the most conspicuous part in the events that have been suggested.

It is necessary to go more into detail. Time began when God announced to the heavenly hosts his decree of begetting the Son and his coronation as the vice-gerent.

> Him have anointed, whom ye now behold
> At my right hand. Your head I him appoint,
> And by myself have sworn to him shall bow
> All knees in Heaven, and shall confess him Lord.
>
> . . . .
>
> . . . Him who disobeys
> Me disobeys, breaks union, and, that day,
> Cast out from God and blessed vision, falls
> Into utter darkness, deep ingulfed, his place
> Ordained without redemption, without end!

The announcement is followed by songs of celebration and praise, but Satan, one of the chief archangels, rebels and becomes the leader of those whom his eloquence and magnetism rally to his side. In the battle that follows, when victory hangs in the balance, the Messiah is sent forth by God to lead the embattled hosts of Heaven. This action is a majestic parallel to the modern hymn "The Son of God Goes Forth to War."

Forth rushed with whirlwind sound
The chariot of Paternal Deity,
Flashing thick flames, wheel within wheel.

. . . .

He, in celestial panoply all armed
Ascended; at his right hand Victory
Sat eagle-winged. . . .

. . . .

He onward came; far off his coming shon.

. . . .

Under his burning wheels
The steadfast Empyrean shook throughout,
All but the Throne itself of God.

When Christ had driven Satan and his hosts through the wasteful deep of chaos to the bottomless pit which had been prepared for them, he returned triumphant into the courts and temples of his mighty Father. Then follows another jubilee in heaven.

To take the place of the fallen angels God sends the Son to create out of chaos the universe, which is to be the home of man. Again he rides forth in splendor and majesty. Heaven opened wide her "ever-during gates" to let forth the King of Glory. To the immeasurable abyss, "outrageous as a sea, dark, wasteful, wild," he says, "Silence, ye troubled waves, and, thou Deep, peace!" With the golden compasses he circumscribes the universe and with his brooding wings sends a vital warmth throughout the fluid mass. This is the birthday of heaven and earth, which is followed by six days of

creation, culminating in the creation of man. Again
Christ is received with jubilation in heaven.

> The great Creator, from his work returned
> Magnificent, his six days' work, a World!

Milton's account of creation is one of the least inter-
esting parts of the poem, although here and there is a
line of true imaginative power. And yet his account has
had a great influence in shaping the ideas of Christian
people. Huxley, commenting on the popular notion of
specific creation with all the details given and inter-
preted by Milton, said that modern scientists, as they
sought to trace the gradual progress of the creative
process, found posted up all over the universe, "No
thoroughfare. By order, Moses and Milton."

When Satan at the end of the council in hell goes
forth upon his great adventure of tempting man and
marring the supernal beauty and order of the uni-
verse, a council in heaven is held, at which God, know-
ing what is going to happen, sets forth the prospect of
the fall and a plan for thwarting the purpose of Satan.
He "argues like a school divine." It is a question as to
whether Milton ought to let God speak at all; he was
less wise than Dante in doing so, but the words of
the Almighty and of the Messiah are the best expres-
sion of what was for a long time the popular theology.
God puts the blame upon man, insisting that he had
free choice and deliberately, without God's predetermi-

nation, would choose evil. "They themselves ordained their fall." The only way out is for someone to pay the penalty of man's sin. The Messiah was filled with compassion as the doom of man was foretold and pleaded with the Father to let him become the ransom, the propitiation for man's sins. God's anger is in sharp contrast with Christ's compassion.

> Behold *me,* then: me for him, life for life,
> I offer; on me let thine anger fall;
> Account me Man: I for his sake will leave
> Thy bosom, and this glory next to thee
> Freely put off, and for him lastly die
> Well pleased; on me let Death wreak all his rage.
>
> .　　.　　.　　.　　.　　.　　.　　.　　.
>
> Father, to see thy face, wherein no cloud
> Of anger shall remain, but peace assured
> And reconcilement: wrauth shall be no more
> Thenceforth, but in thy presence joy entire.

God accepts his offer in words that state even more explicitly the theology that was held alike by Catholics and Protestants of all factions and sects.

After Eve has succumbed to the tempter, and Adam has followed her, and the universe has lost its harmony, the Messiah goes down to Eden. It is here that he becomes most human. The last part of the poem is not generally read; and, it must be confessed, much of it does not attain the high standard of poetic excellence that characterizes the earlier part. And yet it is only in the last three books that Adam and Eve become human beings and that Christ shows the sympathy and tenderness that prophesy his later career on earth. At first Adam and Eve flee from him, where once they had talked with him in the cool of the garden. Adam states the facts of the temptation, and the Messiah passes sentence upon them, announcing that Eve shall bring forth children in sorrow and that Adam shall labor in the sweat of his brow. He leaves them disconsolate, but Adam in the greatest of all his speeches asks questions that remind one of Byron's "Cain."

> Wherefore didst thou beget me? I sought it not!
>
> . . . .
>
> . . . Ah, why should all Mankind,
> For one man's fault, thus guiltless be condemned?

They both long for death, and yet in their common sorrow they are willing to suffer vicariously, each taking the blame and planning how in offices of love they may lighten the other's burden. Their only consolation in the decree of God is that they may crush the head of the serpent, and that they may find in creative work some satisfaction.

Meantime the Messiah returns to heaven and reports their repentance and their resolution to face the future. As a priest he brings before the Father the confessions of the sinners and begs him to accept their words and prayers as a propitiation, and looks forward to the time when the redeemed may dwell in joy and bliss. The Father yields but orders Michael to drive them from the garden. Before the archangel does this, however, he presents to Adam a panoramic vision of the future of mankind—the successive generations of sins, disasters, catastrophes, concluding with the vision of Calvary. The realization of the effect of their sins on mankind brings sorrow to Adam and Eve. But they rejoice in the hope that all this evil will turn to good, that grace will cause man to reach a better state than that of original innocence. Under the inspiration of the Holy Spirit and by reason of the promised Messiah they go forth out of Eden to face a new and different world.

The conclusion of the poem suggests that paradise will be regained, or it leads to that hope. The story has been often told that Thomas Elwood, a close friend of Milton's, said to him when he read *Paradise Lost*, "Why do you not now give us Paradise Found?" whereupon Milton in a few weeks presented to him his poem *Paradise Regained*. In writing *Paradise Lost* he had used Homer and Virgil as his models of epic poetry. In writing *Paradise Regained* he had in mind the book of Job. There are many parallels between the two. In each we have a long-suffering and desolate man face to face with the great temptations of his life. The friends of Job are parallel to Satan in suggesting causes for doubt and in offering ways out of the difficulty. In both works the interest is psychological. The temptations put in the mouth of Satan might well have been in the mind of Jesus. We have the story of a young man just on the threshold of his career, weighing the ideals and values that should dominate his life. He had been formally baptized by John and acknowledged as the Son of God by the descending dove. His mother and his friends were looking to him to free his people from Rome. He himself recalls the time when "victorious deeds flamed in [his] heart" as he thought of rescuing Israel from the Roman yoke and sitting on David's throne.

He is now in the desert, a veritable wasteland, and is hungry after forty days of fasting. The successive temptations of Satan are very real; they are not in any sense a farce. He might have succumbed to any one of them and not been altogether wrong. Why should he not have used his power to turn stones into bread, since he performed the miracle of feeding the multitude? Why should he not adopt the means of political and even military power? It would not be long before his followers would be joining Constantine the Great in his triumphant conquest of Constantinople. Some of the greatest men have worked mightily to meet force with force, to oppose injustice with justice, to win liberty from tyranny. Marcus Aurelius, Pericles, Cromwell, Joan of Arc went that way, why not he? The most subtle temptation Satan puts before him is the charm and beauty and glory of Greek art, philosophy, literature, the city of Athens shining through the centuries— words which expressed Milton's own feeling for the glory that was Greece. Did not Socrates and Plato live almost perfect lives, and did not their teachings become a potent influence through the centuries? Was not the Messiah's most enduring work that of a teacher? And as to the third temptation, were not his miracles the chief argument for his divinity for many people, and has not magic played an important part in the history of all religions?

Careful reading of the poem inevitably raises these questions. The battle is not fought out with a background of heaven or of the Garden of Eden as in the other poem, and for that reason the struggle in the mind of Christ is all the more impressive. Here, you feel, is one of the supreme illustrations of right values and right standards. If he had succumbed to any one of these temptations, in the process of time he would have been surpassed or at least equaled. A great modern scholar and critic would never have been able to say, after a profound study of Plato, "If Plato had lived in the time of Christ, he would have hailed him as his Lord and Master."

With all that may be said for the warriors who have led the crusades of the world, we may still claim that only through love, persuasion, magnanimity may peace be realized on earth. We may still say that greater than any miracle Christ ever performed was the miracle of his life and his love. Milton put something—not all— into this series of temptations. When Christ emerged from the desert and returned to his home, he had become fixed in all his essential ideals. To maintain them he would eventually face the cross.

At the time he was writing *Paradise Lost,* Milton was drawing up a very long statement of the articles of his belief. Strangely enough, the document remained unpublished until 1825, a century and a half after his death. It is a treatise on theology, arranged around certain general subjects, such as God, Christ, sin, and so forth. It is buttressed by many quotations from the Bible. Perhaps no one has been more familiar with every part of the Bible than Milton. The first picture we have of him is that of a boy twelve years old reading the Bible in Hebrew. In all his poems and in his controversial writings he alludes to or uses this vast wealth of material. When he finished his *Treatise on the Christian Doctrine,* he wrote as a preface a letter to all the churches of Christ, which, however, turns out to be the church John Milton himself had organized in the recesses of his own mind. It is the best possible gloss or commentary on *Paradise Lost,* and it shows him to have been far more of a heretic and dissenter than most people who held the orthodox faith had ever imagined. It shows that he repudiated not only Calvin's ideas of predestination and free will but even the doctrine of the Trinity. In the letter he says:

To all the churches of Christ, and to all who profess the Christian faith throughout the world, Peace, and the Recognition of the Truth, and Eternal Salvation in God the Father, and in our Lord Jesus Christ.

Since the commencement of the last century, when religion began to be restored from the corruptions of man those 1300 years to something of its original purity, many treatises of theology have been published. . . . I resolved not to repose on the faith or judgment of others in matters relating to God; but on the one hand, having taken the grounds of my faith from divine revelations alone, and on the other, having neglected nothing which depended on my own industry, I thought fit to scrutinize and ascertain for myself the several points of my religious belief, by the most careful perusal and meditation of the Holy Scriptures themselves.

Referring to the fact that he had been a student of the Bible in the original languages and that he had studied the theologians, who often missed the meaning of passages, he added:

Neither my creed nor my hope of salvation could be safely trusted to such guides, and so I planned some original treatise, designed solely from the word of God. . . . This is my best and richest possession. . . . Many things have been brought to light which will at once be seen to differ from certain received opinions.

Claiming the right of freedom of discussion and inquiry, he appeals to men of mature and manly understanding, as he winnows and sifts every doctrine. He will not be deterred from such freedom "by the imputation of the name of heretic." He closes with an injunction that those who read the letter shall cultivate truth with brotherly love: "Finally, live in the faith of our Lord and Saviour Jesus Christ. Farewell."

The most noteworthy part of this theological treatise is his treatment of Christ as the Son of God. He argues with an abundance of the sayings of Christ himself that he could not be considered as identical with God. "If Christ is God, how can he be the mediator? How can he pray to God?" Christ distinctly disclaimed the attributes of divinity, such as omniscience and omnipotence. Milton is aware that he has accepted the Arian heresy in making this distinction, but he is none the less an ardent believer in the Incarnation and Passion of the Lord. "If I were a Catholic, then my faith would be proscribed, but as a Protestant, I have the right to study the facts." He claims that this belief is more worthy than the creed in general acceptance. He appeals to reason, which is man's highest faculty, to show that the Father and the Son differ in *essence*.

Although *Paradise Lost* has been generally accepted as the epic of the Puritan faith, and was for a long time next to the Bible as an authority on evangelical faith, it can be readily seen that the story of the coronation of the Son in the fifth book and the record of the various conversations between God and the Messiah in the councils of heaven are the imaginative expression of Milton's creed. However much he may have followed the articles of faith in almost every other detail, he aligns himself with the Arians of other times and the Unitarians of a later time.

CHAPTER IX

William Blake:
Rebel and Prophet

LYTTON STRACHEY once said, "Signs are not wanting that the whirligig of time, which left Blake for so long in the Paradise of Fools, is now about to place him among the Prophets."

Emily Dickinson might have had Blake in mind when she wrote:

> Much madness is divinest sense
> To a discerning eye;
> Much sense the starkest madness.
> 'Tis the majority
> In this, as all, prevails.
> Assent, and you are sane;
> Demur,—you're straightway dangerous,
> And handled with a chain.[1]

Wordsworth said that he preferred the insanity of Blake to the sanity of Byron and Scott. Cowper said to Blake one day: "Oh, that I were insane always. Cannot you make me truly insane? You retain health and yet are as insane as any of us. . . . Madness is a refuge from unbelief, from Bacon, Newton, Locke. We are citizens of eternity."

[1] From *The Poems of Emily Dickinson*, edited by Martha Dickinson Bianchi and Alfred Leete Hampson. Used by permission Little, Brown & Co.

119

All of which might lead to a discussion of the ever-mooted question as to whether Blake was insane. It is largely a matter of definition, as is every consideration of aspects of Blake's character and genius. I prefer to agree with Sir Walter Alexander Raleigh, the brilliant Oxford scholar and critic, that Blake "is one of the boldest, most spontaneous, and most consistent of English poets and thinkers." For once I agree with Swinburne, whose dithyrambic praise of some aspects of Blake's writings awakened the minds of many people to the fact that he was one of the greatest of English poets, notwithstanding his many eccentricities and unpardonable faults. Space does not allow me to do more than suggest his influence on many of the outstanding contemporary poets—on Yeats, who said that when one reads Blake, "it is as though the spray of an inexhaustible fountain of beauty was blown into our face"; on Housman, author of *A Shropshire Lad,* who said, "For me the most poetical of all poets is Blake. I find his lyrical note as beautiful as Shakespeare's and more beautiful than any one else's"; on Amy Lowell, who regarded him as a forerunner of Imagism and said, "All eternity shouts in that overborne man for me."

He has had some strange descendants who have regarded him as the forerunner of Nietzsche, Freud, various theosophists, D. H. Lawrence, and Walt Whitman.

Much needs to be said before we consider Blake's interpretation of Jesus. By many he is regarded as a pure mystic, or as the author of those inexpressibly beautiful *Poetical Sketches* and *Songs of Innocence and Experience.* I need not, I am sure, even suggest those short poems that are now in all our anthologies—such as "The Lamb," "The Little Black Boy," "The Chimney Sweeper," "Holy Thursday," "Infant Joy," and their contraries in the *Songs of Experience.* Even here, especially in "The Divine Image" and "The Garden of Love" and "London," there is the presence of his Divine Master. His is a faith as spontaneously held as are the delights of childhood in nature and in animals. Swinburne characterizes with rare felicity his mastery of simple lyric forms:

His songs have the softness of flowers—a sound like the running of water, a ringing of bells in a long lull of the wind, . . . the freshness of clear wind and purity of blowing rain—a perfume as of dew or grass.

These early poems are, after all, but a small part of his complete writings in poetry and prose. It must be admitted that almost any point of view can be proved from the writings and reported conversations of Blake. He was nothing if not paradoxical. He liked to startle people, to shock them by some extravagant turn of expression. His famous saying that "the road of excess leads to the palace of wisdom" is characteristic of his extreme generalizations. The general opinion that the fundamental quality of his mind is his uncompromising rebelliousness may be illustrated in his revolt against

the hypocrisy that parades itself as worship, against
the injustice that miscalls itself law, and against the
make-believe that calls itself religion. He was in re-
bellion against the conventionalities of the pseudoclassic
poetry of the eighteenth century, against the tyranny
of kings and lords, against the authority of priests of
all descriptions, against the popular paintings of Rey-
nolds and Lawrence, against the conventional ideals
of God and Christ, heaven and hell. If you take many
quotations literally, you can see how paradoxical he
was in his thinking. He did not know how to react
from one extreme without going to another. In *The
Marriage of Heaven and Hell* he contends that there is
no such thing as wickedness and at the same time that
you are wicked if you think there is. Some of his "Prov-
erbs of Hell" have been the slogans of his rebellious
descendants. They remind one of Emerson's brilliant
halftruths.

Prudence is a rich, ugly old maid courted by Incapacity.
He who desires but acts not, breeds pestilence.
If the fool would persist in his folly he would become
wise.
Prisons are built with stones of Law, Brothels with bricks
of Religion.
The lust of the goat is the bounty of God.
The nakedness of woman is the work of God.
The cistern contains: the fountain overflows.
As the caterpiller chooses the fairest leaves to lay her
eggs on, so the priest lays his curse on the fairest joys.

Damn braces. Bless relaxes.

Improvement makes strait roads; but the crooked roads without Improvement are roads of Genius.

It is no wonder that Swinburne exalts *The Marriage of Heaven and Hell* as the greatest of Blake's works. There are many other examples of such paradoxical statements. The interpretation of them depends altogether on the context and on the definitions he has in mind. At times he criticizes reason as the "specter of his mythology which like a wild beast guards his way," by which he means the pure intellect divorced from the other faculties of the soul; at other times he magnifies reason when interpreted as reason in her more exalted mood, associated with emotion and imagination. At one time he denounces nature in almost the same terms Tennyson uses in his "Nature, red in tooth and claw"; at other times in his shorter lyrics, as well as in his long "Prophetic Books," he writes some of the most beautiful nature poetry in the language, depicting nature as the revelation of the beauty and wonder and mystery of God. In his attacks on natural religion he condemns science as manifested in Bacon and Newton —"If Bacon was right, Christ was wrong"—and yet elsewhere he calls upon Christians to recognize scientific truth: "He who despairs and mocks a Mental Gift, mocks Jesus, the Giver of every mental gift." He seems at times to degrade woman and to advocate free love, and yet his own happy marriage and many passages in his poems illustrate the sanctity of love. He uses "God" at times as the most cruel term he can command, making him synonymous with Satan, Jehovah, or Zeus; and yet he finds the true interpretation of God in the revelation made by Jesus. As he thinks of what the Church has made of Jesus, he protests against his domination; and yet in the conclusion of *Jerusalem* he celebrates the coming of Jesus into his kingdom as the beginning of a new heaven and a new earth.

One can escape the difficulties of the interpretation of Blake only by considering his writings in their chronological order. There is no doubt that, after he had expressed in memorable verse the innocence and joy of childhood, with something of the same rapture we found in Traherne, he passed through a period when "he faced the spectres of the mind." This is seen first in the contrast between *Songs of Innocence* and *Songs of Experience*—between "The Lamb" and "The Tiger," or the contrasting pictures of London.

When he wrote *The Marriage of Heaven and Hell* and his early "Prophetic Books," he was face to face with the injustice of the world that had found dramatic expression in the French and American revolutions; with the formalism, ceremonialism, and hypocrisy not only of the Roman Catholic Church but of the Anglican and dissenting churches, even with the narrowness of the leaders of the Wesleyan Revival; and just as much with the intellectualism and rationalism of the deists and their natural religion—Bacon, Newton, and Voltaire.

He saw his age cursed with war and with the new industrialism that he symbolized in his "dark satanic mills." Flaming with righteous indignation at all these perversions of the human soul, he appeared as a rebel, a revolutionist. The arrows of his scorn and the sword of his spirit were let loose upon all these forms of perverted life. This is why he called evil so much that was considered good and that had about it the sanctity of established custom and convention, and this is why he called good that which seemed to be at odds with conventional morality and ideas.

But Blake did not stop with mere negation; he was not merely iconoclastic and destructive. After 1800 and on till the end of his life he grew into a maturer view of life and of the world. He recovered a good deal of the spirit of his earlier poems because he came to see that behind the forms and creeds of organized religion there was the spirit of Jesus. In what seems to me a much greater production than *The Marriage of Heaven and Hell* he wrote "The Everlasting Gospel," in which he took up his cudgels against what seemed to him the false conceptions of Jesus. Imperfect and incomplete as the poem is, it is the most illuminating expression of his deeply religious faith.

That this was not simply poetic expression is evinced by letters written at the time he was composing this poem. His letters show, as Plowman says, that Blake was a Christian—"first and last, if not absolutely all the time"—and a Bible Christian.

To John Flaxman, *Oct 19, 1801.*

. . . The Kingdoms of this World are now become the Kingdoms of God & His Christ, & we shall reign with him for ever & ever. . . . Blessed are those who are found studious of Literature & Humane & polite accomplishments. Such have their lamps burning & such shall shine as the stars. . . .

To Thomas Butts, Felpham, *Jany. 10, 1802.*

. . . That I cannot live without doing my duty to lay up treasures in heaven is Certain & Determined, . . . & why this should be made an objection to Me, while Drunkenness, Lewdness, Gluttony & even Idleness itself, does not hurt other men, let Satan himself Explain. The Thing I have most at Heart—more than life, or all that seems to make life comfortable without—Is the Interest of True Religion & Science, & whenever any thing appears to affect that Interest (Especially if I myself omit any duty to my Station as a Soldier of Christ), It gives me the greatest of torments. I am not ashamed, afraid, or averse to tell you what Ought to be Told: That I am under the direction of Messengers from Heaven, Daily & Nightly. . . . Temptations on the right hand & left; behind, the sea of time & space roars & follows swiftly; he who keeps not right onward is lost, & if our footsteps slide in clay, how can we do otherwise than fear & tremble?

To Thomas Butts, Felpham, *Novr. 22, 1802.*

. . . Tho' I have been very unhappy, I am so no longer. I am again Emerged into the light of day; I still & shall to Eternity Embrace Christianity and Adore him who is the Express image of God; but I have travel'd thro' Perils & Darkness not unlike a Champion. I have Conquer'd, and shall Go on Conquering. Nothing can withstand the fury of my Course among the Stars of God & in the Abysses of the Accuser. My Enthusiasm is still what it was, only Enlarged and confirm'd.

From this time on Blake set forth the ideas expressed in these letters. We come now to the consideration of the long poems known as the "Prophetic Books." I must confess I do not understand these books as a whole. Like many others I have tried in vain to work out the complex mythology and cosmogony he invented as the symbols of stories he attempted to tell. He once said that he had to invent a system of his own or be enslaved by another's. With certain basic ideas in his mind he endeavored to find an adequate imaginative form for them. Undoubtedly he saw the vast figures that moved through these books, but he did not have the patience or the constructive ability to fashion them or their background so that even the most intelligent readers can have any definite idea of what it is all about. When Arthur Symons showed certain of Blake's artistic sketches to Rodin and remarked that Blake had seen the figures only once, the French sculptor remarked that it would have been better if he had seen them three or four times.

I feel better for acknowledging my inability to unravel these stories when I think of the experience of other far abler men. Sir Walter Alexander Raleigh spoke of them as a "nightmare, broken by sudden miracles of spiritual insight, and irradiated by wonderful gleams of tender memory. I came to the surface—gasping for breath, confused, bewildered and unconvinced"; and Maria Wilson characterized them as "a smouldering rubbish heap dimly lit by flickering flames of sense and beauty." Swinburne, while he had hopes that sometime someone might find the key that would open the doors of these "multitudinous trances," said that if one would realize what chaos is, "let him take a blind leap into the midst of the whirling foam of this sea of words." Of the titans of monstrous forms and yet more monstrous names he says, "They babble with vast lips a dialect barren of all but noise, loud or loose in the wind."

The amazing thing is that in these chaotic happenings and deeds and persons dimly portrayed there often comes the figure of Jesus. As Schorer says in a recent book, "Jesus is the very keystone of Blake's thinking." From careful study of the texts and of the commentaries by such men as Gardner, Plowman, and Damon, one may summarize the points of view that animate these writings as a whole. Man lived originally in Eden, a world that corresponds to the empyrean of Milton, along with the Council of God and with the Perfect Man Jesus. The Land of Beulah just below Eden corresponds somewhat to the Garden of Eden, in which human beings and gods repose, always with the possibility of returning to Eden. In process of time Albion, a sort of Everyman representing humanity, falls and is found upon a rock in the world of Ulro, a land of darkness, verging upon Nonentity. He reminds one of Job upon his ash heap; he is isolated, hopeless, waiting, it seems, in vain for someone to redeem his lost powers. Four gods, who represent the four faculties of man's soul, were invented by Blake to symbolize the supernatural forces that play about Albion. They too have fallen because they became divided. Urizen represents intellect, Luvah the emotions, Tharmas the body, and Urthona, afterward Los, the spiritual qualities of man. When they were united in his complete personality, Albion was happy and reproduced their variety and unity. The trouble came when Urizen let Luvah take charge of the Chariot of Light, or when the emotions superseded the intellect; intellect, when divorced from other faculties, becomes purely rational. He reduces everything to demonstration and experiment; he peeps and botanizes; he invents natural religion; he doubts rather than believes. Luvah gives full reign to passion, which in turn leads to jealousy and hatred. Urizen is the false God, Luvah the false Christ. The other two figures are not clearly distinguished, but from them springs eventually Los, who becomes an embodiment of spiritual energy that has in it the source of regeneration. These figures and more have their "spectres" and "emanations." The spectre is the knowing cynic, the rationalist, the destructive power, the self-righteous Mr. Worldlywise Man. The emanation is the delighted mind, the pitiful eye, the generous heart, the spirit of affirmation as opposed to doubt. Man himself is torn between these two attitudes.

The chaos that comes from the conflict between all these forces and that is in the mind and heart of Albion is held within the Mundane Shell, which prevents the eternal death of Albion and all those who share with him the utter chaos. Meantime the Council in Heaven is not unmindful of the suffering of Albion. Jesus is sent to become a part of this chaos in the sense that he comprehends it and is able to regenerate man and the universe. In some of Blake's greatest passages we find Jesus as representing the fullness of life: ethically, forgiveness of sins; aesthetically, imagination; socially, the brotherhood of man.

Of all the "Prophetic Books" the most significant are *Milton* and *Jerusalem,* both written over a period of years and brought to completion in the later years of Blake's life. It would be impossible to give any adequate idea of the stories that are supposed to be told in the two poems, for one would be lost in trying to deal with the various characters and their spectres and emanations, while the confusion in the names of the places and in the cosmology would be hopeless. In the first poem he attempts to correct, under the inspiration of Milton himself, whom he saw in a vision, some of the views enunciated in *Paradise Lost,* especially Milton's magnifying of reason as contrasted with the emotions, his stern moral code, and his attributing the debasement of sexual relations to the fall of Adam and

Eve. Blake had always admired Milton, had illustrated several of his poems, and had had visions of him at various times. One vision included Milton's plea that Blake should correct some of the impressions that are gathered from *Paradise Lost;* to save Milton intrigued him. He is represented as making his way out of heaven or Eden, after wandering there for a hundred years, down into the Mundane Shell. The central conflict of the poem is between Milton and Satan. Satan represents the pride of intellect and of doubt, pretending even to have assumed the place of God in the universe. He says to Milton:

I am God the judge of all, the living & the dead.
Fall therefore down & worship me, submit thy supreme
Dictate to my eternal Will, & to my dictate bow.
I hold the Balances of Right & Just & mine the Sword.
Seven Angels bear my Name & in those Seven I appear.
But I alone am God & I alone in Heav'n & Earth
Of all that live dare utter this, others tremble & bow,
Till All Things become One Great Satan, in Holiness
Oppos'd to Mercy, and the Divine Delusion, Jesus, be no
    more.

Milton meets this challenge with these words:

Satan! my Sceptre! I know my power thee to annihilate
And be a greater in thy place & be thy Tabernacle,
A covering for thee to do thy will, till one greater comes
And smites me as I smote thee & becomes my covering.
Such are the Laws of thy false Heav'ns; but Laws of
    Eternity

Are not such; know thou, I come to Self Annihilation.
Such are the Laws of Eternity, that each shall mutually
Annihilate himself for others' good, as I for thee.
Thy purpose & the purpose of thy Priests & of thy
    Churches
Is to impress on men the fear of death, to teach
Trembling & fear, terror, constriction, abject selfishness.
Mine is to teach Men to despise death & to go on
In fearless majesty annihilating Self, laughing to scorn
Thy Laws & terrors, shaking down thy Synagogues as
    webs.
I come to discover before Heav'n & Hell the Self right-
    eousness
In all its Hypocritic turpitude, opening to every eye
These wonders of Satan's holiness, shewing to the Earth
The Idol Virtues of the Natural Heart, & Satan's Seat
Explore in all its Selfish Natural Virtue, & put off
In Self annihilation all that is not of God alone,
To put off Self & all I have, ever & ever. Amen.

The poem ends with the determination of Milton
"to cast off Rational Demonstration by Faith in the
Saviour," to cast off Bacon, Locke, and Newton, and
with the coming of Jesus to put an end to those who
deny the faith and mock at eternal life, so that genera-
tion is swallowed up in regeneration. The reign of Jesus
prepares the way for the Great Harvest and Vintage of
the Nations. The outstanding feature of the poem, how-
ever, is the often quoted lyric poem that strikes the key-
note of what is supposed to be an epic poem. It is one
of the great utterances of Blake. No wonder it has been

sung in Canterbury cathedral and has been adopted more than once as the marching song of the embattled hosts of labor.

> And did those feet in ancient time
>   Walk upon England's mountains green?
> And was the holy Lamb of God
>   On England's pleasant pastures seen?
>
> And did the Countenance Divine
>   Shine forth upon our clouded hills?
> And was Jerusalem builded here
>   Among these dark Satanic Mills?
>
> Bring me my Bow of burning gold:
>   Bring me my Arrows of desire:
> Bring me my Spear: O clouds, unfold!
>   Bring me my Chariot of fire!
>
> I will not cease from Mental Fight,
>   Nor shall my Sword sleep in my hand
> Till we have built Jerusalem
>   In England's green & pleasant Land.

This poem might well have been printed at the beginning of *Jerusalem,* which represents the triumph of Jerusalem over Babylon. It is full of allusions to the book of Revelation and is an anticipation of the new heaven and the new earth which will dawn when the ruins of Jerusalem have been repaired and the reign of Jesus, who is the bridegroom of Jerusalem, begins. Jesus appears to Albion, who is throughout all these narrative poems the representative of fallen humanity.

> Then Jesus appeared standing by Albion as the Good
>   Shepherd.
>
> .   .   .   .
>
> Albion said: "O Lord, what can I do? my Selfhood cruel
> Marches against thee. . . ."
> Jesus replied: "Fear not, Albion; unless I die thou canst
>   not live;
> But if I die I shall arise again & thou with me.
> This is Friendship & Brotherhood: without it Man is Not."
>
> .   .   .   .
>
> Jesus said: "Wouldest thou love one who never died
> For thee, or ever die for one who had not died for thee?
> And if God dieth not for Man & giveth not himself
> Eternally for Man, Man could not exist; for Man is Love
> As God is Love; every kindness to another is a little
>   Death
> In the Divine Image, nor can Man exist but by Brother-
>   hood."

The poem closes with the triumph of both Jesus and Jerusalem, with the "Fountains of Living Waters Flowing from the Humanity Divine," and Albion standing before Jesus in the clouds of heaven among the visions of God in eternity.

> As One Man all the Universal Family, and that One
>   Man
> We call Jesus the Christ; and he in us, and we in him
> Live in perfect harmony in Eden, the land of life,

Giving, receiving, and forgiving each other's trespasses.
He is the Good Shepherd, he is the Lord and master.
He is the Shepherd of Albion, he is all in all,
In Eden, in the garden of God, and in heavenly Jerusa-
    lem.

However confused the poem may be in its many de-
tails, it is a striking fulfillment of Blake's prayer that
the Saviour would pour upon him the spirit of meek-
ness and love, and of his purpose in writing the poem:

> To open the immortal Eyes
> Of Man inwards into the Worlds of Thought, into Eternity.

It is the fulfillment of his call to Jerusalem to

> Recieve the Lamb of God to dwell
> In England's green & pleasant bowers.

More noteworthy because clearer in expression are the
two prose passages—one addressed to the deists and the
other to the Christians—which reveal on the one hand
his everlasting opposition to those who would destroy
the religious spirit by appeals to reason and dogma,
whether they were men like Voltaire and Locke or the
Pharisees of dogma, and on the other hand an eloquent
exposition of what he considered the fullness of the
Christian life. Of the latter he says:

I know of no other Christianity and of no other Gospel
than the liberty both of body & mind to exercise the Divine

Arts of Imagination, Imagination, the real & eternal World of which this Vegetable Universe is but a faint shadow. . . . The Apostles knew of no other Gospel. What were all their spiritual gifts? What is the Divine Spirit? . . . O ye Religious, discountenance every one among you who shall pretend to despise Art & Science! I call upon you in the Name of Jesus! . . . He who despises & mocks a Mental Gift in another, calling it pride & selfishness & sin, mocks Jesus the giver of every Mental Gift. . . . Let every Christian, as much as in him lies, engage himself openly & publicly before all the World in some Mental pursuit for the Building up of Jerusalem.

These quotations can give little idea of the dominance of Jesus in all Blake's longer poems, and yet he is most effective in certain short passages that illustrate his lyric genius.

> God Appears & God is Light
> To those poor Souls who dwell in Night.
> But does a Human Form Display
> To those who Dwell in Realms of day.

Or in a poem expressing the very essence of the Christian faith and its opposite:

> Love seeketh not Itself to please,
>   Nor for itself hath any care,
> But for another gives its ease,
>   And builds a Heaven in Hell's despair.
>
> .   .   .   .
>
> Love seeketh only Self to please,
>   To bind another to Its delight,

136

Joys in another's loss of ease,
And builds a Hell in Heaven's despite.

Blake did not believe at all in the theory of the
Atonement as held by Milton and Donne. It was hor-
rible to him to think of God as demanding the death
of Jesus as a propitiation, or ransom, or substitute for
man's sin. The coming of Jesus was rather the fulfill-
ment of God's yearning toward man, and the redemp-
tion found in these "Prophetic Books" is the theory that
from regeneration man passes into the unity which he
has lost. Christ himself, to view it from another angle,
was the fourfold vision which man in his aspiration may
attain. According to Blake the single vision is that which
comes through the five senses, the purely physical re-
action to nature; the twofold vision is the understanding
acting upon what the senses bring; the threefold vision
is the artistic comprehension, the imagination; and the
fourfold vision is that of the total man reaching the
full glory of spiritual perception. More and more he
came to value imagination as the divinest gift, the
source of all religious insight. Or to put it another
way: science is the bones; reason is the flesh; imagina-
tion, the living form.

In other words, Blake believed that the great need
of man was to find a positive rather than a negative
faith. Salvation was not from hell but toward a full and
complete life. While he agreed with his contemporaries,
Wesley and Whitefield, in the necessity for the new

birth, he did not agree that the fine arts were a hindrance rather than an aid to religion. If the seven devils should be cast out, there might be left an empty room if the soul of man was not filled with objects of beauty and love. This was where he broke with Puritanism. To him the "harmonious expansion of all the powers which make the beauty and worth of human nature" was the best conception of the spiritual life, and to him Jesus was the Redeemer and the Saviour because he was as supreme in the realms of intellect and beauty and refinement as he was in the realm of conduct. A man might obey the Ten Commandments, might fulfill the precepts of morality, and yet be lacking in that spiritual energy which comes from the total man.

Blake's central idea, aside from this, was the forgiveness of sin. No man was perfect, and no man could afford to adopt a condescending attitude of pity toward his fellow men. He once said that he never knew a bad man who did not have his good points. To detect the possibilities of men however ignorant or sinful or helpless was his idea of true religion. It is related of him that one time in reading the parable of the prodigal son he completely broke down when he came to the passage, "But when he was yet a great way off, his father saw him." Blake could go no farther. This was the way he felt toward fallen man; and this, he believed, was the secret of the Christian faith.

For all these reasons Blake magnified Jesus. Alfred Kazin says in his introduction to *The Portable Blake*,

"No Christian saint ever came to be more adoring of Jesus." All other commentators agree. Grierson says, "In Blake's picture Christ is nailed not to a dead but a living tree—not self-restraint and self-denial but love which is freedom and forgiveness." John Gould Fletcher, writing to the same effect, says:

Blake had no God except the god comprehensible to man, the divine spirit of humanity, incarnated historically in Jesus, and capable of reincarnation in Everyman. The vision of Christ which he saw was the most bitter enemy of the vision of Christ which other people saw.

Even Swinburne, pagan as he was, was drawn to Blake's interpretation of Christ:

Where the Creator's power ends, there begins the Saviour's power. The God of this world is a thing of this world, but the Saviour or Perfect Man is of eternity. . . . Through Christ the Lord of liberty came to supplant the bondage of law. In him we have the union of the divine crucified man with the creative power . . . not the assumed humanity of God but the achieved divinity of man, not in-carnation from without but development from within, not a miraculous passage into flesh, but a natural growth into Godhead.

Blake himself anticipated all later interpreters when he put his words into the mouth of God:

I am not a God afar off, I am a brother and friend:
Within your bosoms I reside, and you reside in me.

The climax of this interpretation of Jesus, and indeed of Blake's poetry, is "The Everlasting Gospel," written in 1818 after his "Prophetic Books" were finished. Charles Gardner in his *William Blake, the Man* says that, amid all the troubles which followed him so ruthlessly in the decade before, he turned to the Gospels, not "to find comfort, but to justify himself" in the strange mingling of anger and compassion in his temperament. "He fixed his eyes on the figure of Jesus," whose words he read as he had never read them before. Jesus was not all gentleness, meekness, and humility as the orthodox represented him, nor was he the wrath of God made manifest. He superseded the Mosaic law —set aside the Sabbath, turned the severity of the law for harlots, lived a vagrant life, consorted with publicans and sinners. He was strong like a tiger, but meek like a lamb. "There was in Him a marvelously tender compassion, united with a hot hatred of meanness and hypocrisy." Here was what Blake had been seeking all his life. Slowly, concludes Gardner, Blake saw his life as a mere blot by the side of that resplendent life. Then all resentment died in him. The child spirit returned.[2]

Blake insists in the poem "Moral Virtue" that morality is not Christianity, that Roman virtues were embodied in Caiaphas and Pilate, that Plato and Cicero and the Greek deities inculcated high precepts. As he said in

2 P. 165.

another connection, "If Morality is Christianity, Socrates was the Saviour."

> Then Jesus rose & said to Me,
> "Thy Sins are all forgiven thee."

This is the unique word of redemption and salvation.

> The Christian trumpets loud proclaim
> Thro' all the World in Jesus' name
> Mutual forgiveness of each Vice,
> And oped the Gates of Paradise.

Those who were mere rationalists or interpreters of natural religion joined in crying, "Crucify! Crucify!" and followers of Christ have adopted a creed that is the "Greatest Enemy" of the true Christ.

Blake's careful reading of the Gospels revealed Christ, who at twelve years left his parents in dismay because he was about his Father's business when he met the doctors in the temple, who resisted the allurements of Satan's temptations in the wilderness,

> curs'd Scribe & Pharisee,
> Trampling down Hipocrisy,

drove the money-changers from the temple, and said to Nicodemus, "Ye must be born again."

> Humble toward God, Haughty toward Man,
> This is the Race that Jesus ran.

He would have been just as hard on Priestley, Bacon, and Newton, who taught doubt and experiment as the basis of religion and science—men who "see with, not thro' the Eye."

> Did Jesus teach doubt? or did he
> Give any lessons of Philosophy,
> Charge Visionaries with decieving,
> Or call Men wise for not Believing?

It is evident that Blake makes Jesus in his own image —at once fiercely angry and deeply compassionate— for he combines these denunciations of various types and sins with the gentlest sympathy for the woman taken in adultery. This was the supreme example of his forgiving spirit.

> Mary was found in Adulterous bed;
> Earth groan'd beneath, & Heaven above
> Trembled at discovery of Love.
> Jesus was sitting in Moses' Chair,
> They brought the trembling Woman There.
> Moses commands she be stoned to death,
> What was the sound of Jesus' breath?
> He laid His hand on Moses' Law:
> The Ancient Heavens, in Silent Awe
> Writ with Curses from Pole to Pole,
> All away began to roll:
> The Earth trembling & Naked lay
> In secret bed of Mortal Clay,
> On Sinai felt the hand divine
> Putting back the bloody shrine,

And she heard the breath of God
As she heard by Eden's flood:
"Good & Evil are no more!
Sinai's trumpets, cease to roar!
Cease, finger of God, to write!
The Heavens are not clean in thy Sight.
Thou art Good, & thou Alone;
Nor may the sinner cast one stone.
To be Good only, is to be
A God or else a Pharisee.

.   .   .   .

Still the breath Divine does move
And the breath Divine is Love.

He speaks directly to Mary:

Mary, Fear Not! Let me see
The Seven Devils that torment thee:
Hide not from my Sight thy Sin,
That forgiveness thou maist win.
Has no Man Condemned thee?"
"No Man, Lord:" "Then what is he
Who shall Accuse thee? Come Ye forth,
Fallen fiends of Heav'nly birth
That have forgot your Ancient love
And driven away my trembling Dove.
You shall bow before her feet;
You shall lick the dust for Meat;
And tho' you cannot Love, but Hate,
Shall be beggars at Love's Gate."

Mary responds:

My sin thou hast forgiven me,
Canst thou forgive my Blasphemy?

Canst thou return to this dark Hell,
And in my burning bosom dwell?
And canst thou die that I may live?
And canst thou Pity & forgive?

Yes, there is a new dispensation in the word, for Christ

> ... heals the deaf & the dumb & the Blind.
> Whom God has afflicted for Secret Ends,
> He Comforts & Heals & calls them Friends."
> But, when Jesus was Crucified,
> Then was perfected his glitt'ring pride:
> In three Nights he devour'd his prey,
> And still he devours the Body of Clay;
> For dust & Clay is the Serpent's meat,
> Which never was made for Man to Eat.

And then Blake adds with a touch of humor:

> I am sure this Jesus will not do
> Either for Englishman or Jew.

In the simple faith of this poem Blake lived till his death. The last words to his wife were a fitting conclusion of his life: "I have endeavoured to live as Christ commanded, and I have sought to worship God truly in my own home, when I was not seen of men. You have ever been an angel to me. I will draw you." He then burst into a strong, joyous song.

CHAPTER X

Matthew Arnold:
Wanderer Between Two Worlds

As IN the seventeenth century, religion became the central interest and dominant note in the Victorian period. The development of the scientific movement, which in many cases led to agnosticism and determinism; the triumph of industrialism, which was heralded by many as the beginning of a millennial era based on material values; the application of the scientific method to all spheres of knowledge and especially to the study of the Bible; the emphasis upon a sort of Puritan morality, which was frequently the mask of conventional living and even hypocrisy—all these created a reaction in favor of a more deeply rooted faith. The Oxford movement, the Catholic revival, the Broad-Church movement, the prophetic spirit among those who adhered to no established form of religion—all intensified the interest in such questions as: Who and whence am I? Is there a God, and if so is he to be considered as infinite and eternal energy, a stream of tendency that makes for righteousness, or the Father intimately concerned with the affairs of man? and, from the standpoint of this inquiry, "What think ye of Christ?"

The intellectual and spiritual background of this complex era is not within the scope of this survey. We are concerned here with the effect of all these movements on the interpretation of Jesus. Undoubtedly Matthew Arnold has expressed the pathos and tragedy of modern doubt in such well-known poems as "Dover Beach," "The Scholar Gypsy," and the Obermann poems. What many scientists and rationalists and higher critics accepted with a certain satisfaction filled Arnold with regret and longing as he realized "the sick fatigue, the languid doubt, the strange disease" of modern life, with "its sick hurry, its divided aims, its heads o'ertaxed, its palsied hearts." He felt the full force of the attacks that were made on traditional faiths, but he had a certain nostalgia for earlier ages of faith, and he confidently anticipated another age of faith in the years that lay ahead. Meantime he was wandering between two worlds, the one dead, the other not yet born. In "Obermann Once More" he portrayed in vivid words the decline of Roman civilization and the beginnings of the Christian religion. The hard pagan world had ended in disgust and secret loathing, deep weariness and sated lust, when Christ brought to it a quickening life and faith.

> Oh, had I lived in that great day,
>   How had its glory new
> Filled earth and heaven, and caught away
>   My ravished spirit too!
>
> No thoughts that to the world belong
>   Have stood against the wave

Of love which set so deep and strong
From Christ's then opened grave.

No cloister-floor of humid stone
Had been too cold for me;
For me no Eastern desert lone
Had been too far to flee.

No lonely life had passed too slow,
Where I could hourly scan
Upon his cross, with head sunk low,
That nailed, thorn-crownèd Man.

He follows the triumph of Christianity through the
centuries, but the Renaissance and the French Revolu-
tion and all the tendencies of modern thought have
wrecked the hopes of Christian men and destroyed
even faith in the Resurrection.

Now he is dead! Far hence he lies
In the lorn Syrian town;
And on his grave, with shining eyes,
The Syrian stars look down.

In vain men still, with hoping new
Regard his death-place dumb,
And say the stone is not yet to,
And wait for words to come.

Likewise, as he visits the monastery at Chartreuse,
he feels a yearning for the faith of the old religion, or
for one that might relieve the saddened heart of man.

No, Arnold was never peaceful in his doubt; and, far more than many have realized, he had a minimum faith, such as is expressed in "Rugby Chapel" and in some of his sonnets.

In his prose works, *Literature and Dogma, Saint Paul and Protestantism,* and *God and the Bible,* written not for men established in their faith but for critics and doubters who had been too much affected by the critical study of the Bible, he sought to establish faith in the "secret" and "method" of Jesus. These volumes, written before higher criticism had been established as a legitimate approach to the Bible, sound less radical than when they were published. One may not agree with his rejection of the miracles of Jesus or with his attempt to make real the conception of God by substituting for it the Eternal, but there can be no doubt that he felt very deeply many of the fundamentals of the Christian faith, and that he has written some of the best passages on the personality and mission of Jesus as the founder of a spiritual kingdom. He certainly had the greatest respect for those whose faith was of a traditional character. Meeting a preacher who had been working in the slums of London and seeking to encourage him, he asked him how he fared in such a scene and with such work.

"Bravely!" said he; "for I of late have been
Much cheered with thoughts of Christ, *the living bread!*"

O human soul! as long as thou canst so
Set up a mark of everlasting light,
Above the howling senses' ebb and flow,

To cheer thee, and to right thee if thou roam,—
Not with lost toil thou laborest through the night!
Thou mak'st the heaven thou hop'st indeed thy home.

Again, when he met one who had given up his faith in
God and immortality and considered Christ a mere
man, Arnold said:

Sits there no judge in heaven, our sin to see?

More strictly, then, the inward judge obey!
Was Christ a man like us? *Ah! let us try*
If we then, too, can be such men as he!

This sounds strangely like the words of the Master,
who required no formal acceptance of a creed but said
that, if men would follow him, they would learn of
the doctrine. Arnold's minimum faith, born out of an
intense struggle with doubt and out of an earnest
search for truth, is too valuable an asset to be tossed
aside by those who demand a maximum of dogma.

Along with Arnold we may consider Arthur Hugh
Clough, in whose memory Arnold wrote "The Scholar
Gypsy" and "Thyrsis." In his early life Clough wrote
pastoral poems, but his later poems became touched
with doubt; they took on the troubled note that Arnold
so well expressed. Clough wrote one poem, "Easter

Day," which represents two attitudes toward the resurrection of Jesus. Wandering through the streets of Naples and hearing the Easter bells he laments:

> Christ is not risen, no—
> > He lies and moulders low;
> Christ is not risen!

Joseph did not see him nor the faithful women, nor Peter, nor the two disciples walking to Emmaus.

> Ashes to ashes, dust to dust;
> As of the unjust, also of the just—
> > Yea, of that Just One, too!
> This is the one sad Gospel that is true—
> > Christ is not risen!

Men must eat, drink, and die—"most hopeless, who had once most hope, and most beliefless, that had most believed." When the poet faces this loss of faith in all its reality, he reacts toward faith, and the refrain of the rest of the poem is "Christ is yet risen."

> Though He be dead, He is not dead,
> Nor gone, though fled,
> Not lost, though vanished;
> Though He return not, though
> He lies and moulders low;
> In the true creed
> He is yet risen indeed;
> > Christ is yet risen.

.   .   .   .

Life is yet life, and man is man.
For all that breathe beneath the heaven's high cope,
Joy with grief mixes, with despondence hope.
Hope conquers cowardice, joy grief.

And the Easter bells now ring with joy as they did in
Goethe's *Faust* with the redemption of Margaret.

CHAPTER XI

Alfred Tennyson:
Conqueror of Doubts

TENNYSON had struggles with doubt much like those of Arnold and Clough, but "he fought his doubts and gather'd strength"; he would not make his judgments blind, and the struggle continued with him to the end. But he is, after all, on the side of a triumphant faith. T. S. Eliot in an essay too little read has praised *In Memoriam* as one of the great English poems. "Its technical merit alone is enough to ensure its perpetuity." He even says that we must read every word, for there is never monotony or repetition in the 131 cantos. In view of the reaction of nearly all modern poets against Tennyson it is interesting to hear this praise from one who is quite different in technique and in point of view and who not only hails *In Memoriam* but calls Tennyson a great poet.

He has three qualities which are seldom together except in the greatest poets: abundance, variety, and complete competence. Whatever he sets out to do he succeeds in doing, with a mastery which gives us the sense of confidence that is one of the major pleasures of poetry. His variety of metrical accomplishment is astonishing. He had the finest ear of any English poet since Milton. . . . *Maud* and *In Memoriam* are each a series of poems, given form by the greatest lyrical resourcefulness that a poet has ever shown.

One has scarcely recovered his breath from such statements when he reads the paradoxical statement that *In Memoriam* "is not religious because of the quality of its faith, but because of the quality of its doubt. Its faith is a poor thing, but its doubt is a very intense experience." This judgment is like that of Harold Nicholson, who contends that Tennyson would have been a greater poet if he had developed a certain wild or gypsy spirit that was characteristic of him in his younger days and had not been tamed by the compromises and conventionalities of Victorian ethics. One might imagine a critic of Eliot saying he was a great poet when he wrote *The Waste Land* but not when he wrote *Ash Wednesday*.

It is beyond conception how one can read "The Two Voices" or *In Memoriam* or "Locksley Hall Sixty Years After" or "The Ancient Sage" and not believe that Tennyson ended his struggles with doubt with a clear and definite faith. *In Memoriam* is a series of stepping-stones, what the poet himself called the way of the soul from darkness and despair to the full life. The three reasons he gave for his faith in immortality were that life itself demands a future life; that love would not be love if it did not have in it the germ of immortal love; and that Jesus himself made this faith, which had been expressed by so many great thinkers, a concrete reality.

> Tho' truths in manhood darkly join,
>   Deep-seated in our mystic frame,
>   We yield all blessing to the name
> Of Him that made them current coin;
>
> For Wisdom dealth with mortal powers,
>   Where truth in closest words shall fail,
>   When truth embodied in a tale
> Shall enter in at lowly doors.
>
> And so the Word had breath, and wrought
>   With human hands the creed of creeds
>   In loveliness of perfect deeds,
> More strong than all poetic thought.

In the latter part of the poem when the "fuller minstrel" rings in the new year of a world's hope and faith and peace, the climax is in the line "Ring in the Christ that is to be." There is no doubt what Tennyson means by this; it anticipates new and larger interpretations of Christ when men have realized that he has more authority than either an infallible church or an infallible Bible. Just as the knights of the Round Table took an oath to uphold Christ throughout the world, so the poet regarded him as the realization of the highest manhood and the highest divinity. Undoubtedly Tennyson's conception of the ideal man, found in cantos cix-cxiv, was based on his realization that Jesus embodied those qualities. Other passages in the poem warrant the prologue, which was written last, and which has become one of the most popular modern hymns.

> Strong Son of God, immortal Love,
>   Whom we, that have not seen thy face,
>   By faith, and faith alone, embrace,
> Believing where we cannot prove.
>
> .   .   .   .
>
> Thou seemest human and divine,
>   The highest, holiest manhood, thou:
>   Our wills are ours, we know not how;
> Our wills are ours, to make them thine.

These words were given even greater popular significance when at the end of his life he wrote "Crossing the Bar," which was immediately accepted as one of the great hymns of the English-speaking people, and which the poet demanded should always be printed at the end of any volume of his poetry because it was the climax of his poetry and of his faith.

There is abundant evidence in the *Memoir* by his son Hallam that these poetic expressions came from a faith that never wavered. He said he had given his opinion of Christ in *In Memoriam*. The main testimony to Christianity he found, not in miracles, but in that eternal witness, the revelation of what might be called the mind of God. We are told that he had a measureless admiration for the Sermon on the Mount and for the parables—perfection beyond compare, he called them. He was always amazed, he once said, when he read the New Testament "at the splendour of Christ's purity and holiness and at his infinite pity." Somebody spoke of Christ as a failure. "Do you," asked Tennyson, "call that failure which has altered the belief and the social relations of the whole world?" Two things, he said, were impossible to realize: "the intellectual genius of Shakespeare and the religious genius of Jesus." His son, speaking of his increasing spirituality in his later years, says, "It was in the spirit of an old saint or mystic, and not of a modern rationalist, that Tennyson habitually thought and felt about the nature of Christ." He tells of a conversation between his father and Browning, in which they both agreed

that Christianity with its divine morality but without its central figure of Christ would become cold, and that it is foolish for religion to lose its warmth; . . . that the forms of the Christian religion would alter, but that the spirit of Christ would still grow from more to more.

They wished that the Church of England might embrace, as Christ would have it do, all the great nonconformist sects that love the name of Christ.

CHAPTER XII

Robert Browning:
Champion of Faith

I SHALL always remember with more than usual interest a week in July, 1895, which I devoted to the study of Browning's poems. My experience had been that of most readers of Victorian literature. I had read Tennyson and Arnold, Carlyle and Ruskin, George Eliot and Thackeray, not to mention many lesser lights; but Browning had been to me a mere name. I consoled myself for my ignorance with the customary reflection that he was no artist, only a thinker on high themes, and a very obscure one at that, and so hardly worth serious attention. Finally, however, I began to read his poems, and one Saturday midnight I concluded a week's intensive study of various poems by reading the magnificent lines at the end of *Paracelsus*. I felt that I had discovered a new poet—one whose personality was so interesting, whose genius was so unique, whose dramatic power was so signal, whose view of life was so inspiring that he would furnish material for study and thought in future years.

I shall not in this chapter deal with the characteristic features of Browning's art—with his imagery, his picturesqueness, and above all, his dramatic power. Although half he wrote deserves all the criticism that has been directed to his work as a whole, no one who has studied his poems can deny that he is frequently a supreme artist. I feel, however, that he makes an appeal to a larger class of readers because he was prophet as well as poet, seer as well as artist. His "criticism of life" is everywhere apparent in his works—his love of man, his religious fervor, his enthusiasm for the things of the spirit, his faith in God and soul. Dr. Berdoe, an eminent physician of London and author of *The Browning Cyclopaedia,* tells of his conversion from agnosticism to Christianity by reading the poet's works. He had originally been a Christian, but under the guidance of agnostic teachers he had ceased to believe in the fundamental doctrines of Christianity. Of his restoration to the faith I quote his own account:

It was my good fortune one day to hear a brilliant and powerful lecture by Mr. Moncure D. Conway on Robert Browning's "Sordello." Up to that moment I had read nothing of the works of that poet save the few scraps which appear as quotations, usually from "Rabbi Ben Ezra." On the following day I purchased a set of Browning's works. The first poem I read was "Saul." I soon recognized that I was in the grasp of a strong hand, and as I continued to read "Paracelsus," "Men and Women," and "A Death in the Desert," the feeling came over me that in Browning I had found my religious teacher, one who could put me right on a hundred points which had troubled my mind for many years, and which had ultimately caused me to abandon the Christian religion. By slow and painful steps I found my way back to the faith I had forsaken.

We are struck first with Browning's optimism, and this is what distinguishes him from his contemporaries. One knows but little of the intellectual and religious life of the nineteenth century who has not felt, and sympathized with, the doubt and uncertainty that came to men when new revelations of science and thought were being promulgated, and when the old faith was being attacked from all sides, and serious-minded lovers of truth knew not what to believe. This restlessness and, I may say, gloom are reflected in the poems of Arnold and Clough, as we have seen, and in the novels of George Eliot. To go from them to Browning is to go from those who blindly grope for the light to one to whose soul has come the vision of a great light, and in whose bosom is peace.

Tennyson comes forth from the conflict with a hard-won victory; there are still the traces of the conflict, however, and at times he can but "faintly trust the larger hope." Browning from the very first struck no uncertain note; one sees that the poet feels what is going on about him, but nothing can shake his confidence or destroy his faith. If there is "perpetual unbelief," it is kept quiet "like the snake 'neath Michael's foot who stands calm just because he feels it writhe." If there is doubt, it is only so much as "bade him plant a surer foot on the sun-road."

No one can accuse him of being the shallow optimist Pippa's song would suggest. We shall more and more perceive that Browning felt, as perhaps no other man

in his age did, the real significance of all the movements
of the time, and he saw them in their proper relations.
Even those who have denied his pre-eminence as a poet
have not denied that he had a very wide outlook on
human life and a deep insight into the problems of his
age.

His faith sprang from no trivial consideration of the
problems of life. He felt the force of Strauss's *Leben
Jesu;* but, unlike George Eliot, he had wisdom enough
to see the weakness of his attack on Christianity, and
"A Death in the Desert" is his answer to the German
scholar. He read, as did everybody else, Renan's *Life
of Jesus,* but the rhetoric of the brilliant Frenchman is
answered in the poetry of the epilogue to *Dramatis
Personae.* Browning felt the significance of modern
science. Dr. Berdoe showed how minute was the poet's
knowledge of nature, and how thorough his conception
of scientific thought; but evolution, even if accepted,
could not shake his faith in a creative intelligence back
of nature, and he did not make the mistake that the
period made, that of going to science for instruction on
matters of faith. He says time and again there is a great
world of the moral life of man—man's loves, fears, joys,
and hopes—that science cannot deal with. Browning
was one of the most learned men of his day; so almost
universal was his knowledge that it called forth re-
peated expressions of wonder. But no one who reads
Paracelsus can fail to hear the poet's message to the
men who would solve the problems of life by reference

to the intellect alone. Browning finally saw, as no other English poet, into the beauty of art and the significance of music; but he was as far removed as possible from a refined aestheticism. He interpreted all music and art in the light of the spiritual facts of human life. His whole life gives evidence of consecration of purpose. He was "ever a fighter" for the truth as he conceived it. Conway tells of a tradition that the poet once stopped near an open-air assembly which an atheist was haranguing, and in the freedom of his incognito gave strenuous battle to the opinions uttered. This is very characteristic of Browning. As a man he was always ready to give a reason for the faith he held, and as a poet he gave the weight of his genius to the promulgation of that faith.

In order to be rightly understood, however, I must say that Browning would not be considered an orthodox churchman. He was "too heterodox for the orthodox, and too orthodox for the heterodox." In studying men and women he did not find certain ideas generally taken as the criteria of Christian life playing an important part in the development of character. One does not find him much exercised over higher criticism and evolution, for instance; but he everywhere lays stress on the fundamental facts of the spiritual life—the soul, with its temptations, its struggles with evil, its progress or decline in spiritual power, and its longings for immortal life—on God as a very present help in time of trouble; and on Jesus as the way, the truth, and the life. These high ideals are incentives to his noblest characters, and they come now and then to the surface in the hearts of the most hopeless outcasts. Admitting many of the attacks that have been made on the Christian Church, he yet distinguished, as he says in his essay on Shelley, between churchdom and Christianity; and realizing the many problems of the world about him—"the burthen of the mystery . . . of all this unintelligible world"—he found an answer to man's questionings of the sphinx in the Christian religion. We do not misread his poems when we say that the words of the dying John to his faithful companions are Browning's own.

> I say, the acknowledgment of God in Christ
> Accepted by thy reason, solves for thee
> All questions in the earth and out of it,
> And has so far advanced thee to be wise.

Yes, to Browning, Christ was "very man and very God." He understood the difficulties in the way of accepting this faith; faith would not be, unless there were some mystery mixed with it; spiritual truth is not as self-evident to all as physical law. Neither the mystery of the immaculate conception, nor the problems connected with the authorship of the Gospels, nor the discrepancies of the text could shake his faith in the eternal truth revealed in the Incarnation. After we have considered all these problems, there yet remains for us the indubitable fact of Christ's transcendent life and character—a personality that cannot be explained from a merely human standpoint. When the hero in "Christmas Eve" has left the place where the Göttingen professor was lecturing on Christ, and explaining the origin of the myth as due to the hallucination of his disciples, he considers the question of the divinity of Christ. Christ is of the greatest significance to mankind, not because of the intellectual statement of moral truth, which had been stated by "voices manifold"; not because of his goodness, which would make of him a saint and not a Redeemer; but because of his power to enforce truth with the power of his divine personality. All men have truth within them.

> . . . the truth in God's breast
> Lies trace for trace upon ours impressed.
>
> .   .   .   .
>
> But my fact is,
> 'Tis one thing to know, and another to practice.
> And thence I conclude that the real God-function
> Is to furnish a motive and injunction
> For practicing what we know already.
>
> .   .   .   .
>
> Morality to the uttermost,
> Supreme in Christ as we all confess,
> Why need we prove would avail no jot
> To make him God, if God he were not?
> What is the point where himself lays stress?
> Does the precept run "Believe in good,
> In justice, truth, now understood
> For the first time"?—or, "Believe in me,

Who lived and died, yet essentially
Am Lord of Life"? Whoever can take
The same to his heart and for mere love's sake
Conceive of the love,—that man obtains
A new truth.

Men have in all ages sought to know God—it is the earnest wish of every devout soul. Christ is the answer to that demand of the human soul. He is the "living oracle." In him we have "speech of God writ down," and this fact frees us from the yoke of guessing why God never speaks. Browning revealed above all the love of God to men. In the Pope's monologue in *The Ring and the Book,* where, by general consent, Browning uttered his deepest words on all the problems of man's life and destiny, the Pope speaks of the power and wisdom of God as revealed in nature, and then says:

> There is, beside the works, a tale of Thee
> In the world's mouth, which I find credible:
> I love it with my heart: unsatisfied,
> I try it with my reason, nor discept
> From any point I probe and pronounce sound.
>
> .   .   .   .
>
> Conjecture of the worker by the work:
> Is there strength there?—enough: intelligence?
> Ample: but goodness in a like degree?
> Not to the human eye in the present state,
> An isoscele deficient in the base.
> *What lacks, then, of perfection fit for God*

But just the instance which this tale supplies
Of love without a limit? So is strength,
So is intelligence; let love be so,
Unlimited in its self-sacrifice,
Then is the tale true and God shows complete.
Beyond the tale, I reach into the dark,
Feel what I cannot see, and still faith stands.

In order to understand the full significance of the truth here uttered by the Pope, that of Christ as the revelation of God's love to men, we must be aware of the important part love plays in Browning's conception of life; it is, indeed, with him "the greatest thing in the world." His poems are one long commentary on Paul's words in the thirteenth chapter of First Corinthians. Love as a redeeming and sanctifying force in human life has been set forth by no poet as well as by Browning. Human love is viewed in the light of the eternal nature of man. A being who leaves love out of his life is a failure, unless, as was the case with Paracelsus, he recovers himself before it is too late.

Life, with all it yields of joy and woe,
And hope and fear, . . .
Is just our chance o' the prize o' learning love,
How love might be, hath been, indeed, and is.

Love, he says finely in "Easter-Day,"

repaired all ill,
Cured wrong, soothed grief, made earth amends
With parents, brothers, children, friends!

In the midst of the sorrows and sufferings of this world, love is the light of man's soul. "Love is all, death is naught." This is no mere theory with Browning; it is the guiding principle of his characters—Paracelsus, the hero in *Pauline*, Colombe, Caponsacchi, Pompilia, to mention only a few.

If the love of man for man is a redeeming power in life, much more so would be the love of God, were it only true! Man has power and will, also love; God has power unlimited, and will infinite; has he love? Browning was not satisfied with the eternal and infinite energy that Herbert Spencer found in the workings of nature, though he felt God's power as few men have; he was not satisfied with the stream of tendency that maketh for righteousness that Matthew Arnold found in history, though he has given ample evidence of his faith in the God of our fathers. He demanded also a loving, personal God, who hears man's prayers and comforts his soul. How Browning does cling to that! One who has not noticed the point especially will be surprised to see how many times there is in Browning's poems the cry of man for God in the midst of the perplexities of this life. The hero in *Pauline* has had amid all his years of search for truth one lodestar—"a need, a trust, a yearning after God"—and he cries out impetuously:

My God, my God, let me for once look on thee
As though naught else existed, we alone!

. . . .

                    . . . Even from myself
I need thee and I feel thee and I love thee.
I do not plead my rapture in thy works
For love of thee, nor that I feel as one
Who cannot die: but there is that in me
Which turns to thee, which loves or which should love.

Festus says, as he looks at his dying friend, Paracelsus:

> God! Thou art love! I build my faith on that.
> Even as I watch beside thy tortured child
> Unconscious whose hot tears fall fast by him,
> So doth thy right hand guide us through the world
> Wherein we stumble.

The two supreme facts in Browning's faith were his belief in his own soul and in the love of God—"he at least believed in soul, was very sure of God." God is after all the supreme fact in the teaching of Christ. Christ continually lost himself in the Father. Browning never loses sight of the Father, as so many have done; but at the same time he says over and over again that men would not know of the Father except through Christ. "Does God love? And will ye hold that truth against the world?" Yes, says Browning, if Christ is true.

> When man questioned, "What if there be love
> Behind the will and might, as real as they?"
> He needed satisfaction God could give
> And did give, as ye have the written word.

By this life and revelation the finite love is blended and embalmed with the eternal life. "The love, the patience, the fidelity, the truth, the long-suffering, the heart of the Infinite and Eternal Energy comes to its fruition and its manifestation in this one incomparable life." God enters into a human life and fills it full of himself that he may show his love for the world. With what new significance do those often repeated words come to us: "God so loved the world, that he gave his only begotten Son, that whosoever believeth in him should not perish, but have everlasting life." Browning would not have interpreted these words, as so many have, by making them refer altogether to the death of Christ; to him the life of Christ was of more significance than his death, though this death was the climax to his life, and the ideal expression of love. Remarkable is the speech of Pompilia, in which she says, as she thinks of her newborn babe:

> I never realized God's birth before—
> How he grew likest God in being born.
> This time I felt like Mary, had my babe
> Lying a little on my breast like hers.

We have thus seen the reason for Browning's faith in Christ. Had he left us nothing but these passages, we should have known his attitude to religious questions. Fortunately, however, he has expressed the idea of the Incarnation in several of his poems that show the working of this faith in the hearts of men. Space will not allow us to consider all of the characters who have faith in Christ, nor all of the passages where Christ is spoken of; we shall only notice the poems where the Incarnation is the central theme; and in this series of poems, some of them his very best from an artistic standpoint, we find a fervent love of and faith in Christ, paralleled only by the early Christians. It is all the more significant that he has represented the Incarnation from so many different standpoints—that of the Greeks and Hebrews in anticipation of it, that of Karshish and John in actual contemplation of its mysteries, and that of the nineteenth-century thinker in "Christmas Eve" and "Easter-Day."

Very few men have entered so sympathetically into the life of the ancient Greeks—their art, their literature, their philosophy. By means of that charming character Balaustion he makes us feel again the glory of Athens, "the life and light of the whole world worth calling world at all"; we feel the presence of the "tragic triad of immortal fame," and hear those "great plays that had long ago made themselves wings to fly around the world." And yet he was not Greek-intoxicated, as Arnold was; nor as Keats, who was really a Greek who found himself out of place in the nineteenth century. Browning was a critic of their life as well as a lover; he interpreted their highest thoughts in the light of Christianity, and saw that they were reaching out for the truth, as all readers of Plato must feel. He criticizes their art in comparison with medieval Christian art, because the invisible was not brought into play.

In the Pope's monologue he represents Euripides as a ghost, speaking to the Pope of all he had attempted to teach—of the high ideals of virtue, love, and duty he had set before the minds of the Greeks, ideals that many Christians do not attain. Then he says:

> How nearly did I guess at what Paul knew?
> How closely come, in what I represent
> As duty, to his doctrine yet a blank?
>
> . . . .
>
> You have the sunrise now, joins truth to truth,
> Shoots life and substance into death and void.

No wonder he could not descry sunshine at midnight, when he "crept all-fours."

In the poem "Cleon" we see this yearning of the Greek mind for "more life and fuller" most clearly set forth. The poet takes Paul's words at Mars' Hill, "as certain also of your own poets have said," as the keynote to this interesting study. Cleon is a finished product of Greek civilization; he is musician, sculptor, philosopher (he has written three books on the soul); all arts are his. And yet, as he grows older, he is discontented, and his soul cries out to Zeus "to indicate his purpose in our life." Is it possible that, while nature improves, the soul alone deteriorates? The soul craves opportunities for unlimited joy. A man can use but a man's joy, though he sees God's. As his sense of joy grows more acute, his soul more enlarged, his vision more keen, his body decays. Then he cries out almost impetuously:

> It is so horrible,
> I dare at times imagine to my need
> Some future state revealed to us by Zeus,
> Unlimited in capability
> For joy, as this is in the desire for joy.
>
> . . . .
> . . . But no!
> Zeus has not yet revealed it; and alas,
> He must have done so, were it possible!

Then Browning, by a subtle irony, lets us know that Cleon has heard of Paul, and yet he is not troubled much to know him:

> Thou canst not think a mere barbarian Jew
>
> . . . .
> Hath access to a secret shut from us?

Paul was then preaching the truth his soul longed for.

More important than the passages which treat somewhat argumentatively and dogmatically the dogma of the Incarnation is Browning's representation of certain dramatic situations and personalities that lead to the expression of Christian faith. In "Karshish" he represents a scientist going through Palestine, making certian observations for his master, an Arab physician. He writes daily notes, recording types of plants that may be of value in curing certain diseases. He spends a night in Bethany, the home of Martha and Mary, where he hears the strange story of the physician who raised Lazarus from the dead. He does not want to appear interested in the story at all, for his master will think he has been taken in by the superstition of the people. So he sends his epistle by a runaway slave whom he has befriended, thinking that it will not matter if it is never received. It is really a matter of no importance, and he turns aside from it now and then to make some comment on a plant or an animal that has scientific value or interest. All the while you feel, however, that he has been strangely affected by the story of Lazarus, whom he meets in person, and who tells him of the man who seemed to be a combination of mystic and healer. He could not find this strange man because he had recently died, but he hears that he claimed to be God himself,

> Creator and sustainer of the world,
> That came and dwelt in flesh on it awhile!

At last Karshish can no longer suppress his interest as he exclaims:

> The very God! think, Abib; dost thou think?
> So, the All-Great, were the All-Loving too—
> So, through the thunder comes a human voice
> Saying, "O heart I made, a heart beats here!
> Face, my hands fashioned, see it in myself!
> Thou hast no power nor mayst conceive of mine,

But love I gave thee, with myself to love,
And thou must love me who have died for thee!"
The madman saith He said so: it is strange.

Thus does Browning dramatically set forth the incompleteness of science in revealing spiritual truth, but the greatest of his poems dealing with the Incarnation is "Saul," in which he reveals—again in a dramatic way—the incompleteness of the Hebrew revelation of God. The poem represents Saul as a fallen and ruined man, whom David, the young shepherd, is using every means to arouse from despair. Through his harp he reveals the beauty of scenery and the glory of animals, to which he has been accustomed.

God made all the creatures and gave them our love
    and our fear,
To give sign, we and they are his children, one family
    here.

He recalls to Saul the folk songs of the Hebrew race, culminating in the songs of the temple. He chants the glory of the physical life that Saul knew as a young man, the wild joys of living.

How good is man's life, the mere living! how fit to
    employ
All the heart and the soul and the senses forever in
    joy!

He creates a vision of Saul's family and the friends of his boyhood—"that boyhood of wonder and hope" which culminated in his selection as king—all the gifts of life "brought to blaze on the head of one creature." When these memories fail to touch the heart of Saul, largely because of the contrast of his present situation, he holds out to him the hope of his living forever in the life of the Hebrew people, the hope that was one of the dominant notes of Hebrew faith. Saul will always be remembered as the first king in the long line of rulers.

When David reaches this point, Saul is somewhat touched but still full of doubt and despair as to his own personal rejuvenation. David then begins to think as he has never thought before about God; he has believed in a God of power and a God of wisdom, but neither will satisfy the need of man. He ventures into a new realm of spiritual thought. Browning was justified in representing him as feeling out after a God of love in that the fifty-third chapter of Isaiah and the book of Job had expressed the same yearning for a human God, one who would reveal himself as suffering with man and as redeeming man. David would give his life for Saul because he has honored and loved him as his king, but does God feel the same way toward man? As he shrinks from the idea that he might surpass God in this one respect, the truth suddenly bursts upon him that God, who had created man, would surely complete his revelation by loving him.

> Would I suffer for him that I love? So wouldst thou—
> so wilt thou!

So shall crown thee the topmost, ineffablest, uttermost
   crown—
And thy love fill infinitude wholly, nor leave up nor down
One spot for the creature to stand in! . . .

.   .   .   .

As thy Love is discovered almighty, almighty be proved
Thy power, that exists with and for it, of being Be-
   loved!
He who did most, shall bear most; the strongest shall
   stand the most weak.
'T is the weakness in strength, that I cry for! my flesh,
   that I seek
In the Godhead! I seek and I find it. O Saul, it shall be
A Face like my face that receives thee; a Man like to me,
Thou shalt love and be loved by, forever: a Hand
   like this hand
Shall throw open the gates of new life to thee! See
   the Christ stand!

If it is urged that the poems which have been cited
are merely dramatic poems, and that we cannot take
them as expressing the poet's own faith, we know from
Browning's letters that he was a sincere believer in the
Christian faith. He said:

I know all that may be said against it on the ground of
history, of reason, or even moral sense. But I am not the less
convinced that the life and death of Christ, as Christians
apprehend them, supply something which humanity re-
quires. . . . Love could only reveal itself to the human
heart by some supreme act of human tenderness and devo-
tion: the fact or fancy of Christ's cross or passion could
alone supply such a revelation.

Further evidence is in the epilogue to *Dramatis Personae*, in which he represents David as speaking in behalf of Israel, when people gathered only at stated times in the temple to rejoice in the worship of God. The second speaker is Renan, who tells of the loss of faith in Christ in modern times—the star of Bethlehem has vanished from the heavens. Then Browning himself speaks, saying that the walls of the world are God's temple and that the star of Bethlehem has not vanished from the heavens.

> That one Face, far from vanish, rather grows,
> Or decomposes but to recompose,
> Become my universe that feels and knows!

Browning said to Mrs. Sutherland Orr, his biographer, one day as he finished reading this poem, "That's the way I feel Christ."

CHAPTER XIII

Nineteenth-Century American Poets

AMERICAN poets were not as disturbed by the scientific and critical trends of modern thought as were some of the Victorian poets. The New England poets reacted strongly against the iron creeds of Puritanism and Calvinism and even against orthodox Unitarianism. The fire-and-brimstone sermons of Jonathan Edwards and Michael Wiggleworth's "Day of Doom" gave way to Emerson's "Over-Soul," Longfellow's *Christus*, Whittier's "The Eternal Goodness," and Lowell's "The Vision of Sir Launfal." Holmes shot many an arrow of his wit at the older creeds, especially satirizing them in "The One-Hoss Shay." So much had been said of original sin and total depravity that the poets emphasized man's natural goodness and culture as the basis of a deeper religious faith. It was natural that the commercial or legal view of Christ's death should have given way to the revelation of his mercy and goodness, his humanity. The poets especially applied the spirit of Christ to the problems of their own times. And yet they were all so related to the traditional moral standards of the old New England—some of them the descendants of a long line of New England preachers—that they preserved the essential spirit of the gospel of

177

faith and works that had characterized the New England of two centuries before. One may claim that "no other group of singers was ever in any country in the same length of time so deeply religious in thought, so uniformly reverent in feeling or tone."

William Cullen Bryant, who is chiefly remembered as the author of the somewhat melancholy "Thanatopsis," belonged to a family in which the Bible was read daily and family prayers were held. His biographer, John Bigelow, says that "though habitually an attendant upon the ministrations of the Unitarian clergy when they were accessible, no one ever recognized more completely or more devoutly the divinity of Christ." Although he did not become an active member of the church until late in life, he wrote several short poems that expressed the faith found in "To a Waterfowl," the faith that God would guide him aright in all the ways of life. He believed that the star of Bethlehem would shed "a lustre pure and sweet" over the world. He looked forward to the time when Christ

> Shall reign from pole to pole,
> And be the Lord of every human soul,

and when all would heed the words he spoke,

> And, by the loving life he led,
> Shall seek to father them;
> And He who conquered death shall win
> The nobler conquest over sin.

Emerson's "Divinity Address," delivered before the Divinity School of Harvard University, was quite as revolutionary as "The American Scholar" of the year before. He maintained the two cardinal ideas that he was to develop in various forms in his later poems and essays: the spirit of God as the source of all man's emotions and ideas, and the dignity and moral worth of the individual soul in communion with God. To him inspiration was universal, and the great danger of traditional creeds was that they were a substitute for the immediate and personal revelation of God to man. Rites, ceremonies, and creeds were of no avail unless they were means to an end. Jesus was the supreme embodiment of these fundamental ideas.

Jesus Christ belonged to the true race of prophets. He saw with open eye the mystery of the soul. Drawn by its severe harmony, ravished with its beauty, he lived in it, and had his being there. Alone in all history he estimated the greatness of man. One man was true to what is in you and me. He saw that God incarnates himself in man, and evermore goes forth anew to take possession of his World. He said, in this jubilee of divine emotion, "I am divine. Through me, God acts; through me, speaks. Would you see God, see me; or see thee, when thou also thinkest as I now think." . . . Thus is he, as I think, the only soul in history who has appreciated the worth of man.

The trouble was, according to Emerson, that this personality of Jesus with his fundamental belief had become a mere tradition, and in many cases a myth. Men substituted a creed about Jesus for their own personal realization of the actual presence of God in their souls. Tradition characterized the preaching of this country; it came "out of the memory and not out of the soul." "It is the office of a true teacher to show us that God is, not was; that He speaketh, not spake."

The fact is that Emerson underrated sin as a fact of life, and consequently did not feel the need of the redeeming power of Jesus for himself or for others. His giving up the ministry because he could not administer always in a conventional way the Holy Communion was characteristic of his attitude to rites, ceremonies, and institutions, and to the historic Christ.

Longfellow, on the other hand, was much concerned with the faith of past ages. It is a striking fact that his two longest works—the translation of the *Divina Commedia,* and *Christus: A Mystery*—were the result of many years of study and reflection. Notes in his diary show that from 1841 until the publication of the complete work in 1873 his greatest ambition was to interpret in *Christus* the life and teachings of Jesus and their effect on later ages. On November 19, 1849, he wrote: "And now I long to try a loftier strain, the sublimer song, whose broken melodies have for so many years breathed through my soul in the better hours of life, and which I trust and believe will ere long unite themselves into a symphony not all unworthy the sublime theme." On January 10, 1850, he wrote: "In the evening, pondered and meditated upon sundry scenes of *Christus.* In such meditations one tastes the delight of the poetic vision, without the pain of putting it into words." The great theme haunted him while he struggled to bring his poem to a satisfactory conclusion. It is composed of three parts: "The Divine Tragedy," a dramatic representation of the incidents of the life of Christ, most of it in the very words of the Gospel; "The Golden Legend," which revealed the faith of the Middle Ages as it manifested itself in the romantic story of Prince Henry and Elsie, in the life of the monks in the monasteries, in the miracle plays on the Nativity, and in the early triumphs of Christianity in Italy and Germany; and "The New England Tragedies," in which the real spirit of Christianity was seen at work in the struggles of Christian saints at the time of the persecution of the Quakers and the hanging of the witches.

The poem as a whole is a failure, although there are passages in the first part—such as the presentation of Mary Magdalene, the interview with Nicodemus, and the story of the Passion Week—that rival the best of Longfellow's poems. Perhaps the best comment on the three parts as a whole is in the words of John at the end as he is represented wandering over the face of the earth during all these periods of history.

> The clashing of creeds, and the strife
> Of the many beliefs, that in vain
> Perplex man's heart and brain,

Are naught but the rustle of leaves,
When the breath of God upheaves
The boughs of the Tree of Life,
And they subside again!
And I remember still
The words, and from whom they came
Not he that repeateth the name,
But he that doeth the will!

And Him evermore I behold
Walking in Galilee,
Through the cornfield's waving gold,
In hamlet, in wood, and in wold,
By the shores of the Beautiful Sea.
He toucheth the sightless eyes;
Before him the demons flee;
To the dead He sayeth: Arise!
To the living: Follow me!
And that voice still soundeth on
From the centuries that are gone,
To the centuries that shall be!

The climax of all the long years he gave to the study
of Dante is found in the sonnets that he wrote as intro-
ductions to *Divina Commedia,* and the best of these is
the one which served as an introduction to the "Para-
diso," the celebration of Christ's triumph as revealed in
the rose window and in the Holy Communion.

I lift mine eyes, and all the windows blaze
With forms of Saints and holy men who died,

Here martyred and hereafter glorified;
And the great Rose upon its leaves displays

Christ's Triumph, and the angelic roundelays,
With splendor upon splendor multiplied;
And Beatrice again at Dante's side
No more rebukes, but smiles her words of praise.

And then the organ sounds, and unseen choirs
Sing the old Latin hymns of peace and love
And benedictions of the Holy Ghost;
And the melodious bells among the spires
O'er all the house-tops and through heaven above
Proclaim the elevation of the Host!

But it is not only in these longer poems that Long-fellow shows his interest in Christian faith. Throughout all his shorter poems and in *Evangeline* there is the spirit of the gentler side of Christianity. He himself said, "I love that view of Christianity which sets it to the tune of a cheerful, kind-hearted friend, and which gives its thoughts a noble and liberal turn." Even when there is no direct reference, the poems are shot through and through with the Christian spirit. He identifies in "Arsenal at Springfield" his attitude to war with that of the voice of Christ, "like a bell, with solemn, sweet vibrations" saying "Peace!"

Peace! and no longer from its brazen portals
    The blast of War's great organ shakes the skies!
But beautiful as songs of the immortals,
    The holy melodies of love arise.

In a poem written for the ordination of his brother, Samuel Longfellow, who afterwards wrote the poet's biography, he quotes the words of Christ to the rich young man and adds:

> Within this temple Christ again, unseen,
>   Those sacred words hath said,
> And his invisible hands to-day have been
>   Laid on a young man's head.
>
> And evermore beside him on his way
>   The unseen Christ shall move,
> That he may lean upon his arm and say,
>   "Dost thou, dear Lord, approve?"
>
> . . . .
>
> O holy trust! O endless sense of rest!
>   Like the beloved John
> To lay his head upon the Saviour's breast,
>   And thus to journey on!

Other Christian poems are his "Christmas Bells," "Noël," *Michael Angelo,* and a translation from the Spanish entitled "Coplas de Manrique."

James Russell Lowell, unlike Longfellow, was primarily interested in political and social problems, but in various poems he showed the effect of religious tradition in his thinking. In the "Present Crisis" he identifies his sense of freedom and of truth with the spirit of Christ. In the poem he rises above the bitterness of some of his antislavery poems and gives permanent expression to the eternal conflict between truth and error, good and evil.

By the light of burning heretics Christ's bleeding feet I
    track,
Toiling up new Calvaries ever with the cross that turns
    not back,
And these mounts of anguish number how each genera-
    tion learned
One new word of that grand *Credo* which in prophet-
    hearts hath burned
Since the first man stood God-conquered with his face
    to heaven upturned.

In each crisis "worshippers of light ancestral make the
present light a crime," while there is need to catch the
light of campfires that lead on to the future.

In "The Search" he recites his experiences in seek-
ing Christ. He sought him first among the kings, amid
power and wealth, but found no trace of him as he
brought his costly offerings. He finally finds him in a
rude hovel with a naked hungry child about his knees
and a poor hunted slave seeking his freedom.

    I knelt and wept: my Christ no more I seek,
    His throne is with the outcast and the weak.

This theme was developed more fully in "The Vision
of Sir Launfal," which may be considered a new ver-
sion of the quest of the Holy Grail, comparable to Ten-
nyson's poem of that name. The setting, however, is an
American one with a well-known description of a June
day at the beginning of the poem and a description of

the winter in the second part. The poem is so well known that it is scarcely necessary to analyze it; suffice it to say that one who in his youth had started upon his journey and not noticed the leper by the castle gate returns in old age "an old, bent man, worn out and frail." A leper is again at the gate begging for alms, and this time Sir Launfal sees in him "an image of Him who died on the tree." Responding to the appeal for help he has a vision of Christ, who says to him:

> In many climes, without avail,
> Thou hast spent thy life for the Holy Grail;
> Behold it is here,—this cup which thou
> Didst fill at the streamlet for me but now;
> This crust is my body broken for thee,
> This water His blood that died on the tree;
> The Holy Supper is kept, indeed;
> In whatso we share with another's need;
> Not what we give, but what we share,—
> For the gift without the giver is bare;
> Who gives himself with his alms feeds three,
> Himself, his hungering neighbor, and me.

Lowell, like Longfellow, felt the charm of the old world. In his "Godminster Chimes," written "in aid of a chime of bells for Christ Church, Cambridge," he has the same emotions Longfellow did when he heard the belfry of Bruges, suggesting the Easter morn when Christ for all shall be risen and in all hearts newborn.

> When all shall say *My Brother* here,
> And hear *My Son* in heaven!

In "The Cathedral," a longer poem of his later years,
he tells his experiences in spending a day at Chartres,
which impressed him much as it did Henry Adams at
a later time. For one time in his life he realized the
meaning of prayer as he had known it "at that best
academe, a mother's knee." The music of the organ,
the beauty of Gothic architecture, the glory of stained-
glass windows gave him a sense of an ancient faith
which culminates in his vision:

> The Cross, bold type of shame to homage turned,
> Of an unfinished life that sways the world,
> Shall tower as sovereign emblem over all.

There is no such passage in Oliver Wendell Holmes,
who rebelled against Calvinism, as he saw it embodied
in his orthodox father and in ministers who visited his
home, to such an extent that he lost his reverence for
ancestral faith. Indeed, by reason of "The .One-Hoss
Shay" and many passages in his prose works he was
considered by the orthodox as another Voltaire. And
yet he wrote two poems, "A Hymn of Trust" and "A
Sun-day Hymn," that have become almost universally
used by members of all denominations. He once said
that his whole creed was summed up by the beginning
of the Lord's Prayer—Our Father—and in these poems
he gives monumental expression to this faith. The
"Hymn of Trust" can only be interpreted in the light of
his faith in the revelation of God through Christ.

O Love Divine, that stooped to share,
   Our sharpest pang, our bitterest tear,
On Thee we cast each earth-born care,
   We smile at pain when Thou art near.

Of all this group of poets Whittier was the sincerest and most passionate in his faith in Christ as his Saviour and Redeemer. He knew nothing of the support of faith that came to Longfellow and Lowell from past ages. He was a descendant of several generations of Quakers and became the foremost interpreter of that quiet, simple, and devout people. From his boyhood he attended their meetings; the meetinghouse impressed his imagination more than any cathedral, for he found his cathedral in the woodland aisles of the New England autumn. Not Dante but Burns was the chief inspiration of his poetry, for he too felt the romance underlying familiar places; his parallel to "The Cotter's Saturday Night" was "Snow-Bound," which is saturated with the spirit of a pious New England home. Worship with his family, his neighbors, and his friends was fully described in the poem entitled "The Meeting."

I ask no organ's soulless breath
To drone the themes of life and death,
No altar candle-lit by day,
No ornate wordsman's rhetoric-play,
     .   .   .   .
No pulpit hammered by the fist
Of loud-asserting dogmatist,

188

Who borrows for the Hand of love
The smoking thunderbolts of Jove.

.   .   .   .

I reverence old-time faith and men,
But God is near us now as then.

.   .   .   .

So, where is neither church nor priest,
And never rag of form or creed
To clothe the nakedness of need,—
Where farmer-folk in silence meet,—
I turn my bell-unsummoned feet.

Many of his poems reveal and interpret the humbler men and women who made up the congregation of Quakers. The best of these is a characterization of a Pennsylvania Quaker who came from Germany to find his home with the followers of Penn. Learned in several languages, a lover of nature, a missionary to the Indians, and one of the leaders of his meetinghouse,

Within himself he found the law of right,
He walked by faith and not the letter's sight,
And read his Bible by the Inward Light.

.   .   .   .

His was the Christian's unsung Age of Gold,
A truer idyl than the bards have told
Of Arno's banks or Arcady of old.

But Whittier was more than the poet of the Quakers. In his poems "The Eternal Goodness" and "Our Master" he wrote two of the great religious poems of all times—poems that have universal value as expressions of the Christlike spirit. In the first poem he protests the logic "linked and strong" of the iron creeds; his heart pleads for the goodness and love of God.

> I walk with bare, hushed feet the ground
>   Ye tread with boldness shod;
> I dare not fix with mete and bound
>   The love and power of God.
>
> Ye praise His justice; even such
>   His pitying love I deem;
> Ye seek a king; I fain would touch
>   The robe that hath no seam.
>
> Ye see the curse which overbroods
>   A world of pain and loss;
> I hear our Lord's beatitudes
>   And prayer upon the cross.

His faith will not attribute to God qualities that are not even up to the human level of goodness.

> Not mine to look where cherubim
>   And seraphs may not see,
> But nothing can be good in Him
>   Which evil is in me.
>
> The wrong that pains my soul below
>   I dare not throne above,
> I know not of His hate,—I know
>   His goodness and His love.

I dimly guess from blessings known
  Of greater out of sight,
And, with the chastened Psalmist, own
  His judgments too are right.

The poem ends with the words of confident faith in immortality that have sung themselves into the hearts of thousands of believers.

And so beside the Silent Sea
  I wait the muffled oar;
No harm from Him can come to me
  On ocean or on shore.

I know not where His islands lift
  Their fronded palms in air;
I only know I cannot drift
  Beyond His love and care.

O brothers! if my faith is vain,
  If hopes like these betray,
Pray for me that my feet may gain
  The sure and safer way.

And Thou, O Lord! by whom are seen
  Thy creatures as they be,
Forgive me if too close I lean
  My human heart on Thee!

The Eternal Goodness is, of course, God, but God as interpreted by the mind and heart of Christ. "Our

Master" is a direct and definite expression of his vivid sense of the presence of the Master, who is

> No dead fact stranded on the shore
>   Of the oblivious years;—
> But warm, sweet, tender, even yet
>   A present help is he;
> And faith has still its Olivet,
>   And love its Galilee.

We realize his present existence by ministering to beds of pain and by touching him in life's throng and press. He is "the flower of man and God," for he reveals the fatherhood and heart of God. Contrary to much popular theology there is no distinction between the Father and the Son, no rivalry between the Cross and the Throne.

> Thy litanies, sweet offices
>   Of love and gratitude;
> Thy sacramental liturgies,
>   The joy of doing good.

> In vain shall waves of incense drift
>   The vaulted nave around,
> In vain the minister turret lift
>   Its brazen weights of sound.

No wonder he exclaims:

> Immortal Love, forever full,
>   Forever flowing free,

Forever shared, forever whole
A never-ebbing sea!

Sidney Lanier was most like Whittier in his passion-
ate faith. Reacting from the strict Presbyterian environ-
ment and training of his early days, he found a fuller
and larger faith as he devoted himself to music and to
poetry. In a poem called "Remonstrance" he protested
strongly against "the prim Creed, with categoric point"
that sought to feature his Lord by "rule and line." Jesus
was deeper than any line could sound. No rubric, no
hairsplitting test of creed, no desire even of lovers to
think alike, could shake his tolerant spirit. He cries
upon opinion to let him alone. It might be an assassin,
a thief. Christ alone could deliver men from bondage
and make them free to live with love, and give them a
faith that would find his presence in the stars above,
the clods below, the flesh without, the mind within. In
"Acknowledgment" Lanier characterizes the age as one
that half believes and half doubts.

Yea, if the Christ (called thine) now passed yon street,
    Thy halfness hot with His rebuke would swell;
Legions of scribes would rise and run and beat
    His fair intolerable Wholeness twice to hell.

In "How Love Looked for Hell" he represents Sense
and Mind as showing him hell, but Love can find no
place where men are without hope—they have dreams,

they talk of grace, they repent even in the midst of their sins.

But Lanier was not satisfied to stop with a negative point of view. In "The Symphony" he anticipated much modern thought about industrial problems. He represents the various stringed instruments of an orchestra protesting against modern trade and the spirit of commercialism. The strife of fierce competition, the mean-got gains of rich men, the oppression of labor are set over against the words of Christ, such as "Man shall not live by bread alone," "Love thy neighbour as thyself," "Except ye . . . become as little children, ye shall not enter into the kingdom of heaven." Two of the most powerful protests are against child labor and the degradation of woman by commercialism. All the chivalry and kindliness and tenderness of Lanier come out in this poem, and they have their explanation in his thorough assimilation and championship of the Christian faith. It is not an exaggeration to say that the spirit of love which he invoked is identical with the spirit of Christ, and it is not straining the point to say that the conclusion is an expression of this point of view.

> And ever Love hears the poor-folks' crying,
> And ever Love hears the women's sighing,
> And ever sweet knighthood's death-defying,
> And ever wise childhood's deep implying,
> But never a traitor's glozing and lying.

And yet shall Love himself be heard,
Though long deferred, though long deferred:
O'er the modern waste a dove hath whirred:
Music is Love in search of a word.

No one has entered the poignant tragedy of Gethsemane better than Lanier, whose poem "A Ballad of Trees and the Master" has become one of the favorite expressions of the emotions of Passion Week.

Into the woods my Master went,
Clean forspent, forspent,
Into the woods my Master came,
Forspent with love and shame.
The thorn-tree had a mind to Him
The little gray leaves were kind to Him:
The thorn-tree had a mind to Him
When into the woods He came.

Out of the woods my Master went,
And He was well content.
Out of the woods my Master came,
Content with death and shame.
When Death and Shame would woo Him last,
From under the trees they drew Him last:
'Twas on a tree they slew Him—last
When out of the woods He came.

In "The Crystal" he characterizes the defects and limitations of the great men of history—Buddha, Socrates, Epictetus, Shakespeare, Milton, and others—and closes with an apostrophe to Jesus as the perfect crystal. Emerson mentions in one of his poems "Plato's brain," "Shakespeare's strain," and "Lord Christ's heart" as equal manifestations of the Over-Soul. Not so Lanier!

> But Thee, but Thee, O sovereign Seer of time,
> But Thee, O poets' Poet, Wisdom's Tongue,
> But Thee, O man's best Man, O love's best Love,
> O perfect life in perfect labor writ,
> O all men's Comrade, Servant, King, or Priest,—
> What *if* or *yet*, what mole, what flaw, what lapse,
> What least defect or shadow of defect,
> What rumor, tattled by an enemy,
> Of inference loose, what lack of grace
> Even in torture's grasp, or sleep's, or death's,—
> Oh, what amiss may I forgive in Thee,
> Jesus, good Paragon, thou crystal Christ?

CHAPTER XIV

Francis Thompson:
Poet from the Slums

DURING the last days of the Victorian era there was a revival of Roman Catholicism in England and America —a frontal assault upon the stronghold of the faith of Anglicans and of various other forms of Protestantism. "The second spring," of which Cardinal Newman had written some of his most eloquent words, meant the revival in England of the Catholic Church after centuries of repression and persecution. Neglected shrines and altars were revived, heirlooms that had been preserved in the mansions of Catholic noblemen were resurrected, monasteries in all parts of England were housing nuns and priests. The words of Cardinal Newman were inspiring younger men, and the administration of Cardinal Manning was bringing about a more efficient organization. In the salon of Wilfrid and Alice Meynell many converts and others who were temporarily susceptible to a faith that counteracted some of the decadence manifested in aesthetic circles—such men as Lionel Johnson, William Watson, Stephen Phillips, Wilfred Blunt, Oscar Wilde, and even W. B. Yeats in his younger days—often met. Coventry Patmore was the link between the Victorians, for whom he had written *The Angel in the House*—an almost perfect expression of the domestic ideals of the age—and this younger group of poets.[1]

Somewhat apart from this group was Francis Thompson, who after living for several years as an outcast on the streets of London was received into the home of the Meynells as friend and brother. They made for him a home and inspired his earliest poems, which were published in *Merry England,* a magazine edited by Wilfrid Meynell with the purpose of stirring up enthusiasm for the Christian ideals that had prevailed in England before the Reformation.

Breaking away from his home in Manchester after failure to satisfy Catholic divines that he was fitted for the ministy and after an attempt to prepare himself for the practice of medicine, Thompson had repeated the experience of De Quincey by roaming the streets of London, doing every sort of menial job to assuage his hunger, and finally taking laudanum as a relief from his pains. He had veritably fallen under the dominion of the Mother of Tears, the Mother of Sighs, and the Mother of Darkness until he was saved in a moment of contemplated suicide by the Madonna. Truly it might have been said, as was said of De Quincey and of Dante, "This man had been in hell!"

Imagine the contrast between such a life and that which the Meynells and their children opened up to

[1] See further George N. Shuster, *The Catholic Spirit of Modern English Poetry.*

him. Alice Meynell, a poet as well as a most gracious hostess, was characterized by Richard Le Gallienne:

> Never surely was a lady who carried her learning and wore the flower of her gentle humane sanctity with such quiet grace, with so gentle and understanding a smile. The touch of exquisite asceticism about her seemed but to accent the sensitive sympathy of her manner. . . . There was the charm of a beautiful abbess about her, with the added *esprit* of intellectual sophistication. However quietly she sat in her drawing-room of an evening with her family and friends about her, her presence radiated a peculiarly lovely serenity, like a twilight gay with stars. . . . I have no other such picture of a full and harmonious home life to settle by its side.[2]

Her patience, her understanding, and her belief in Thompson made her a veritable ministering angel, an earthly madonna, in the life of this strange and unconventional poet. As one of the editors of *The Academy* wrote:

> A stranger figure than Thompson's was not to be seen in London. Gentle in looks, half-wild in externals, his face worn by pain and the fierce reactions of laudanum, his hair and straggling beard neglected, he had yet a distinction and an aloofness of bearing that marked him in the crowd. . . . A clearer mind, a more naïvely courteous manner, were not to be found. . . . His great brown cape, which he would wear on the hottest days, his disastrous hat, and his dozen neglects and makeshifts were only the insignia

[2] Viola Meynell, *Alice Meynell*, p. 143.

of our "Francis." . . . From a newness too dazzling to last
. . . he passed at once into a picturesque nondescript garb
that was all his own and made him resemble some weird
pedlar or packman. . . . Unembittered, he kept his sweet-
ness and sanity, his dewy laughter, and his fluttering grati-
tude. In such a man outward ruin could never be pitiable
or ridiculous, and, indeed he never bowed his noble head
but in adoration. I think the secret of his strength was this:
that he had cast up his accounts with God and man, and
thereafter stood in the mud of earth with a heart wrapt in
such fire as touched Isaiah's lips.[3]

Suddenly and dramatically from these surroundings
came, one year after the death of Tennyson, "The
Hound of Heaven," which produced a sensation in a
period of decadence because of its blending of the sad
tragedy of a poet's life with the buoyant faith of one
who had found in God a refuge and a consuming love.
Young poets like Walter de la Mare shouted it as they
walked the streets of London. Arnold Bennett hailed
Thompson as having "a richer natural genius, a finer
poetical equipment than any poet save Shakespeare";
and a brilliant young journalist greeted him, "A rarer,
more intense, more strictly predestinate genius has
never been known to poetry." Since then the poem has
become recognized as one of the great poems of the
modern age and as one of the supreme expressions of
religious faith. It is so well known that it does not call
for quotation. It may seem strange that God, or rather

[3] *Ibid.*, p. 222.

Christ, should be pictured as a hound in search of game. Like all figures or symbols it needs to be seen as a very venturesome expression of a deep religious truth. The emphasis is on God's quest for man rather than man's quest for God. It is a parallel to Emerson's "Brahma," and especially to the line, "When me they fly, I am the wings." It is an extended poetical interpretation of the passage in the Psalms, "Whither shall I go from thy spirit? or whither shall I flee from thy presence?" The point is that nothing can satisfy the soul of man—no beauty, no friendship, no parental love, no pleasure. If he becomes contented with any finite thing, he becomes dead to the demands of his infinite and ultimate nature.

But this poem is only one of a group in which Thompson expresses more definitely his faith in Jesus. He undoubtedly had faith in the Virgin and depended upon more than one saint. He was especially influenced by Cardinal Manning and called upon him to plead for him in the court of heaven. He leaned upon Coventry Patmore, who visited him in the monastery in Wales. He celebrated the English martyrs, by whose blood they "held in fee the future of England." In the midst of his suffering on the streets of London he found Jacob's ladder, "pitched between heaven and Charing Cross"; he saw Christ walking on the waters, "not of Gennesaret, but Thames." In a criticism of Milton he spoke of him as a poet to whom all might bow the knee, few or none the heart. But to Thompson, Christ was associated with his deepest emotions. His "Little Jesus" is as simple and childlike as Blake's "The Lamb."

He was one of the first Englishmen to realize the significance of the Salvation Army and of General Booth's *In Darkest England*. He wrote a powerful review of the book because he had lived in the slums and through the experiences Booth described. "If Christ stood amid your London slums he could not say, 'except ye become as one of *these* little children.'" He saw, as did Cardinal Manning, that the Church needed to profit by the spirit and methods of the Salvation Army. He insisted, however, that there should be substituted "for the discipline of trumpets, the discipline of the Sacraments; for the chiming of tambourines, Mary's name like a bell-tongue in men's resonant souls."

In many other poems Thompson expressed his faith in Jesus. Taking the mass at sunrise, he emphasizes in his "Orient Ode" the sun as a symbol of salvation— "Yon orbèd sacrament," which sprinkles benediction through the dawn. The sun is both destroyer and preserver; it demands law in that it holds the planets in place, but it is also a symbol of sacrificial love.

> Thy proper blood dost thou not give [to earth].
>
> . . . .
>
> Art thou not life of them that live?
>
> . . . .
>
> The victim daily born and sacrificed;
>
> . . . .
>
> To thee, O Sun—or is't perchance to Christ?

In his "Ode to the Setting Sun" he describes a remarkable sunset, in connection with which he saw reflected Calvary—a "dreadful pomp of blood." He suggests that the sun sets on earth to rise in heaven, and thus becomes an emblem of faith in immortality as well as an emblem of the sacrifice of the cross. In "The Veteran of Heaven" he represents a meeting with the Saviour, grievously wounded.

> O Captain of the wars, whence won Ye so great scars?
> In what fight did Ye smite, and what manner was the
> foe?

The Saviour answers:

> Twas on a day of rout they girded Me about,
> They wounded all My brow, and they Smote Me
> through the side:
> My hand held no sword when I met their armèd horde,
> And the conqueror fell down, and the Conquered
> bruised his pride.

> .   .   .   .
> . . . My name ye may not know;

> .   .   .   .
> But My titles that are high, are they not upon My thigh?
> "King of Kings!" are the words, "Lord of Lords!"

In other words, Thompson finds in Jesus what William James called "the moral equivalent of war," and he is ready to enlist under his banner.

CHAPTER XV

Gerard Manley Hopkins:
Jesuit Scholar

ANOTHER poet who passionately expressed the Catholic faith was Gerard Manley Hopkins, who came to the faith under very different circumstances from Thompson—from the university rather than from the streets. At Oxford he had come under the influence of all the currents of thought of his age. Called by Jowett "The Star of Balliol" because he was the greatest scholar of his generation of students, he had as tutor Walter Pater, who at that time was exercising considerable influence in the direction of Epicureanism and aestheticism. Hopkins sympathized with Ruskin's efforts to introduce art into the life of England. He felt the appeal of Arnold for culture as a solution of England's problems.

In short, "all shores of learning extended before him like the shores of beckoning continents." But the voice that sounded the most compelling notes was that of Newman, whose autobiography appeared in 1864, while Hopkins was at Oxford. He recaptured the mood that had taken Newman to the Roman Catholic Church.

After correspondence and several interviews with Newman he was received into the church, choosing the Jesuit order as his form of service rather than the

Benedictine. It is said that no one has ever taken more seriously the "spiritual exercises" of that order—the stages through which one must pass to find ultimate peace. With rare sincerity and honesty he determined to realize in his own life all the meanings of Catholic symbols and ceremonies, and especially to re-enact in his own life the Incarnation and the Redemption. He subjected himself to dark rooms, fasting, and mortification of the body. While others might seek to magnify the church and the sacraments, he made the supreme object of his life to be like Christ, *alter Christus*. "Beautiful was Christ's life, but a billion times lovelier was his self-immolation on the cross." His sacrifice was transmuted by the fire of love into something far greater than any natural beauty. All his feeling for beauty merged in "the rarer beauty, the grace of God." Hopkins sought in every way to examine his conscience, to meditate, to pray orally and mentally, in order that thereby he might better visualize and realize Christ. Robert Bridges, editing a volume of Hopkins' poems twenty years after his death, struck the keynote of his poetry when he said that the "love of Christ will win man's love at last."

The first thing Hopkins did after he had passed through his purgation in the monastery was to burn all the poems he had written. He was then silent for seven years, believing that the writing of poetry would interfere with his priestly career. But when he read the account of the wreck of the "Deutschland" and the drowning of five Franciscan nuns who were exiled from Germany and on their way to America, he was so deeply stirred that, at the suggestion of one of his superiors in the monastery, he wrote his passionate poem "The Wreck of the Deutschland." The pent-up flood waters were at last released by the bursting of the dam, and seven years of religious life became articulate.

The passionate faith of the poem is matched by the revolutionary quality of the verse, the explosive words coming in shifts of accent—"sprung rhythm" is the technical term—which has greatly influenced his successors in poetry. "I had long had haunting my ear the echo of a new rhythm which now I realized on paper" was his expression of this technique. The poem is difficult to read because of its contractions, its omission of connecting words, its irregular feet, and its bold and passionate leapings from image to image. But one who reads it carefully, with some aid in the way of interpretation, will be convinced that it is one of the most original and most powerful poems in the English language. The narrative itself is in stanzas 12-17—a breathtaking account of the loss of two hundred who fought with God's cold sea and winds, with "the sea-romp over the wreck." He singles out one of the nuns, who arose "breasting the babble," "a prophetess towered in the tumult"—towering because of her faith and her sacrificial spirit—a sister calling a master, "her master and mine."

... There then! the Master,
Ipse, the only one, Christ, King, Head:
He was to cure the extremity where he had cast her.

. . . .

Jesu, heart's light,
Jesu, maid's son,
What was the feast followed the night
Thou hadst glory of this nun?—
Feast of the one woman without stain.
For so conceivèd, so to conceive thee is done;
But here was heart-throe, birth of a brain,
Word, that heard and kept thee and uttered thee outright.

But the significance of the poem is not so much in
the narrative of this heroic event as in its effect on the
poet himself. While living in Wales "under a roof in
the loveliest west," he realized the fierce intensity of the
incident. Here he felt the finger and presence of Christ.
He had heard of him in Augustine and Francis of As-
sisi, but here was the truth revealed in his own age—
Christ as lightning and rod, terror but also love. The
hero of Calvary explains the heroism of the nun—"the
Christ of the Father compassionate, fetched in the
storm of his strides." He has learned from experience
what it means to dedicate himself entirely to the service
of Christ, but he also sees the significance of faith in
modern England, as he exclaims:

Our King back, oh, upon English souls!
Let him easter in us, be a dayspring to the dimness of us,
be a crimson-cresseted east,

More brightening her, rare-dear Britain, as his reign rolls,
Pride, rose, prince, hero of us, high-priest,
Our hearts' charity's hearth's fire, our thoughts' chivalry's
throng's Lord.

Hopkins realized that other articles in the Catholic
faith were necessary. He wrote perhaps the best state-
ment of the place of the Virgin Mary in one's faith. She
is like the air or the atmosphere, which at once veils the
brighter light of the sun and produces colors that add to
the beauty and strength of faith in Jesus.

So God was god of old:
A mother came to mould
Those limbs like ours which are
What must make our daystar
Much dearer to mankind;
Whose glory bare would blind
Or less would win man's mind.
Through her we may see him
Made sweeter, not made dim,
And her hand leaves his light
Sifted to suit our sight.

The Virgin is further celebrated in the poem "The
May Magnificat," in which she is represented with all
the beauty of the springtime. The ceremonies of the
church are best described in "The Bugler's First Com-
munion," with its haunting expression of the idea of
transubstantiation. The priest fetches from the cup-
board Christ himself and gives him to his youngest

recruit, and is glad to serve to "just such slips of soldiery" Christ's royal ration. At another time he identifies the courage and faith of the soldiers with that of Christ himself. His is not merely the pacifist Christ, for he represents the Master as saying, "Were I come o'er again, it should be this—a Christ-done deed."

But beyond the Virgin or the symbols is Christ himself.

> In a flash, at a trumpet crash,
> I am all at once what Christ is, since he was what I am.

And again:

> Jesu whom I look at shrouded here below,
> I beseech thee send me what I thirst for so,
> Some day to gaze on thee face to face in light
> And be blest forever with thy glorious sight.

In his later years at the University of Dublin he passed through what the mystics call "the dark night of the soul." Ill health, the drudgery of reading innumerable examination papers, his separation from England, the uncongenial atmosphere of a university which failed so signally to realize the dream of Newman—all these produced a profound melancholy. He was a stranger among strangers. He passed through "wearying, wasting, wasted years." He had sacrificed all to the priesthood, even any right that he might have to win recognition or fame by the publication of his poetry.

He felt that, to be a priest and to carry out to the extreme the spiritual exercises he had so thoroughly mastered, he must reproduce the very passion of Christ. He felt the truth of what Thomas à Kempis said: "Jesus hath many lovers of his heavenly kingdom, but few of his cross. Many follow Jesus with the breaking of bread; but few to the drinking of the cup of his passion." He came to a state of "spiritual dryness," "interior desolation." His last sonnets were written as in blood. In one of them he talks straight into the face of the Master, reminding one of the pathetic and tragic words of Job on his ash heap. Just as he had asked the Comforter where was the comfort and the Mother where was her relief ("Carrion Comfort"), so now he addresses the Master directly, after he had wrestled in the dark with his God.

> Thou art indeed just, Lord, if I contend
> With thee; but, sir, so what I plead is just.
> Why do sinners' ways prosper? and why must
> Disappointment all I endeavour end?
> Wert thou my enemy, O thou my friend,
> How wouldst thou worse, I wonder, than thou dost
> Defeat, thwart me? Oh, the sots and thralls of lust
> Do in spare hours more thrive than I that spend,
> Sir, life upon thy cause. See, banks and brakes
> Now, leavèd how thick! lacèd they are again
> With fretty chervil, look, and fresh wind shakes
> Them; birds build—but not I build; no, but strain,
> Time's eunuch, and not breed one work that wakes.
> Mine, O thou lord of life, send my roots rain.

It is no wonder that Aldous Huxley said of this poem, "Never has the just man's complaint against the universe been put more forcibly, nor more tensely and fiercely." It is like the cry in the Garden of Gethsemane or on the cross. And yet Hopkins never lost his faith; to the end he tried to realize that his suffering was not to be compared with that of Christ, whose "plans were baffled, his hopes dashed, and his work done by being broken off, undone." After much physical and spiritual struggle during those last years he died with the words upon his lips, "I am so happy, so happy."

CHAPTER XVI

Contemporary Poets
1. T. S. Eliot

ONE OF the most remarkable facts in modern religious history is that Eliot, born in St. Louis and inheriting the blood of New England Puritans, should have in the process of time become for England the best voice of the High-Church element in the Anglican church. I need not recite the stages by which he came to his belief that the Anglo-Catholic church was the rock in the somewhat stormy and tempestuous sea of modern life and thought. In his early poetry he voiced better than anybody else the disillusionment and desolation that had come as the result of what Walter Lippmann calls "the acids of modernity." Unintelligible as most of the poem is, the title and some of the lines of *The Waste Land* phrase the symbolism of utter desolation that follows the loss of faith. In "The Hollow Men" we have the same sort of expression in a different figure— men as cynics and pessimists have brought our world where it goes down, "not with a bang but a whimper." The Church itself is represented in the hippopotamus, with its machine-like organization and its formalism "wrapped in the old miasmal mist."

Somehow Eliot has found his way out of this chaos

and confusion to a very definite faith in the Anglican form of creed and worship. In his plays *Murder in the Cathedral* and *The Rock* and in shorter poems such as "Journey of the Magi," *Ash Wednesday*, and "A Song for Simeon" he has represented some of the more poignant aspects of the life of Christ and the history of the church. Does not one feel, however, that he was more concerned about the Church than about the person of Jesus Christ? His faith is the result of thought rather than of emotion or experience. This does not mean that he has not been honest in his beliefs, but no such personal experience as we found in Donne or Browning or Hopkins has played its part in his evolution toward faith. He is such a believer in the technique of metaphysical poetry that the reading of him has been difficult for the general public, although it has meant much that a man of such attainments has found necessity in our modern world for Christian faith. Some who hailed him as a great poet in the early stages of his career have looked upon him as a lost leader because he has reacted to a more conservative point of view, not only in religion but in politics and in literary criticism.

A few passages suggest his religious insight. He resents the statement of John A. Hobson that "the barbaric sense of the exceeding sinfulness of sin, with the mere hatred it carried is giving away to a more natural attitude," that "vice offends more from its ugliness than from its sinfulness," and that "goodness has its appeal

in moral beauty rather than in virtue." On the other
hand Eliot insists that the modern world has

Knowledge of speech, but not of silence;
Knowledge of words, and ignorance of the Word.
All our knowledge brings us nearer to our ignorance,
All our ignorance brings us nearer to death,
But nearness to death no nearer to GOD.
Where is the Life we have lost in living?
Where is the wisdom we have lost in knowledge?

And again:

The cycles of Heaven in twenty centuries
Bring us farther from GOD and nearer to the Dust.
.   .   .   .
Men have left GOD not for other gods, they say, but for no
    god; and this has never happened before
That men both deny gods and worship gods, pro-
    fessing first Reason,
And then Money, and Power, and what they call Life. . . .
The Church disowned, the tower overthrown, the bells
    upturned, what have we to do
But stand with empty hands and palms turned upwards
    In an age which advances progressively backwards?

After this indictment he closes *The Rock* with an apos-
trophe to the Light Invisible:

We thank Thee for the lights that we have kindled,
The light of altar and of sanctuary;
.   .   .   .
And lights directed through the coloured panes of
    windows
And light reflected from the polished stone.

And when we have built an altar to the Invisible Light,
we may set thereon the little lights for which our
bodily vision is made.
And we thank Thee that darkness reminds us of light.
O Light Invisible, we give Thee thanks for Thy great
glory!

Here and there we are made aware of the presence
of Christ in all the symbolic and ceremonial aspects of
religion

And the Son of Man was not crucified once for all,
The blood of the martyrs not shed once for all,
The lives of the Saints not given once for all:

Has the Church failed mankind, or has mankind failed
the Church?

Son of Man, behold with thine eyes, and hear with
thine ears.

LORD, shall we not bring these gifts to Your service?

Now you shall see the Temple completed:
After much striving, after many obstacles;

The dressed altar, the lifting light,
Light
Light
The visible reminder of Invisible Light.[1]

In his *Murder in the Cathedral*, which was written
for production at the Canterbury Festival, June, 1935,

[1] Used by permission Harcourt, Brace & Co., Inc.

and was acted at the Mercury Theatre in London in January, 1936, Eliot sets forth dramatically the conflict between Thomas à Becket and his enemies. Thomas had in his earlier days been worldly in his ambition and in his deeds; and his tempters, the messengers of the king and of the established church, remind him of his former glory and hold out the hope of still greater glory. He accepts the role of martyrdom, refusing even to put up a semblance of a fight at the doors of the cathedral when the murderers are upon him. He says that the church is not a fortress, and he is willing to give his life as a sacrifice to the law of God above the law of man. He will conquer by suffering: "Now is the triumph of the cross." He is a Christian, saved by the blood of Christ, "ready to suffer with my blood." Christ's blood was given to buy his life; his blood is given to pay for this death—"my death for his death." After he has paid the supreme sacrifice, the chorus sings the *Te Deum*. The Church is stronger for this action—"triumphant in adversity."

> For wherever a saint has dwelt, wherever a martyr has
> given his blood for the blood of Christ,
> There is holy ground, and the sanctity shall not depart
> from it.[2]

The play ends with a prayer for mercy to God, to Christ, and to the "Blessed Thomas." [3]

[2] Used by permission Harcourt, Brace & Co., Inc.
[3] For further comment see ch. i, pp. 23, 27-29.

2. John Masefield

Some readers will remember the sensation in literary circles when John Masefield published in *The English Review* "The Everlasting Mercy." [4] This was a poem that came straight out of the heart, not of the Catholic or Anglican churches, but the same evangelical churches that had produced Bunyan and Milton in one generation and the Wesleys in another. It is the story of the prodigal son in the language of a very different world. Saul Kane for ten years had broken his mother's heart in two; for ten years he had followed women and wine, and for six years had rationalized his conduct by his doubts and positive atheism. There is a climax of dissipation at the village pub about Easter time. The bells of the church waken in him only scorn, for he "shut out Christ in husks and swine." The words of an old woman, telling him of what ruin he has wrought in the community and especially on children like her own boy, and the realization of the havoc he has caused in the lives of young women make him realize his life of sin. A Quaker maiden speaks to him:

> "Saul Kane," she said, "when next you drink,
> Do me the gentleness to think
> That every drop of drink accursed
> Makes Christ within you die of thirst,
> That every dirty word you say

Is one more flint upon His way,
Another thorn about His head,
Another mock by where He tread,
Another nail, another cross.
All that you are is that Christ's loss."

When he left the pub, something broke inside his
brain as he went out into the darkness.

The bolted door had broken in,
. . . .
I knew that I had done with sin.
I knew that Christ had given me birth
To brother all the souls on earth.
. . . .
O glory of the lighted mind,
How dead I'd been, how dumb, how blind.

All nature now takes on the rapture of his joy: the
brook "babbling out of Paradise," "God's eternal gar-
den flowers," "the dawn with glittering on the grasses,"
"the white-blossomed pond." He feels that "Heaven's
gate was opened wide," and the past fades like a dream.
The common scenes of the farm take on new glory as
he turns to his work once more. He calls upon Christ
to plow his heart as he plows the ground; he greets the
Easter morning:

O lovely lily clean,
O lily springing green,
O lily bursting white,
Dear lily of delight,
Spring in my heart agen
That I may flower to men.

Masefield afterward wrote a Good Friday play and a play entitled *The Coming of Christ,* but he has never recaptured the art or the glory of that first careless rapture.

3. Vachel Lindsay

Two years later in Harriet Monroe's magazine *Poetry* there appeared Vachel Lindsay's "General William Booth Enters into Heaven," which was at once an expression of the Salvation Army's revival spirit and the inauguration of a new era in American poetry. It could have been written only by a man who in his early days had attended many revival meetings held by the followers of Alexander Campbell, had sung the old-fashioned community hymns, had witnessed the conversion of many people, and had in his visits to Chicago and New York realized the meaning of this new expression of evangelical faith and passionate reformation that had swept through the English-speaking world under the leadership of General Booth. The form of the poem shows also Lindsay's mastery of jazz music at its best and of homely, vigorous language.

The refrain of the poem is an echo of the revival meetings he attended in earlier days—"Are you washed in the bloom of the Lamb?" It contains vivid pictures of those who followed in Booth's train—"walking lepers," "lurching bravos," "drabs from the alleyways," "vermin-eaten saints"—from every slum around the world. The climax is his being received by Jesus in heaven.

> And when Booth halted by the curb for prayer
> He saw his Master thro' the flag-filled air.
> Christ came gently with a robe and crown
> For Booth the soldier, while the throng knelt down.
> He saw King Jesus. They were face to face,
> And he knelt a-weeping in that holy place.
> Are you washed in the blood of the Lamb? [5]

Seven years before this, while he was coming home from a visit to Europe, he saw and heard a vision of Immanuel. This was based on a famous popular song. Lindsay, following the example of the Negro spirituals, found words appropriate to the melody. By his directions given in the margin of the poem "I Heard Immanuel Singing" one can feel the blending of popular music and poetry. The vision and the melody were so real to him that the words convey the impression of the Incarnation and the Redemption. Jesus combined the shepherd David and Apollo of the Silver Bow.

> I saw Immanuel singing
> On a tree-girdled hill.
>
> . . . .
>
> The grand new song proclaiming
> The Lamb that had been slain.
> New-built, the Holy City
> Gleamed in the murmuring plain.

[5] From *Collected Poems* (copyright 1925, The Macmillan Co.). Used by permission the publishers.

All these he sang, half-smiling
And weeping as he smiled,
Laughing, talking to his harp
As to a new-born child:—
As though the arts forgotten
But bloomed to prophecy
These careless, fearless harp-strings,
New-crying in the sky.[6]

Thus early did Lindsay come to associate music and poetry and to realize the place of Jesus in our democracy. When he wrote his *Golden Book of Springfield* and the shorter poem "The Building of Springfield," he saw the Christian Church as a mighty factor in his dream city. Christ the beggar would teach divinity, and beautiful parks and art galleries would express his spirit. He once wrote of the Christ spirit giving for humanity its choicest gifts—"I have supreme faith in Christianity as a social force." To have faith in God and to love Christ with fervor was his ideal for a Christian. To him Christ was the creator, the scientist, the poet, the philosopher, the statesman. "I can build a chapel in my heart to the Christ," he once said, "that is, in other men, or the religion of humanity."

He felt that the appeal of Christ was universal because there were so many sides to his nature.

The substance of Christian Science might account for his healing. . . . The substance of Catholicism is suggested by

[6] From *Collected Poems* (copyright 1925, The Macmillan Co.). Used by permission the publishers.

his assertion of authority, this transference of authority to the apostles. The substance of pantheism is suggested by his desert prayer. . . . His nature parables, his roadside bohemianism, his epicureanism by his interest in publicans and sinners. . . . His asceticism by his single life and pure teachings. . . . His socialism by his Sermon on the Mount.

4. Edwin Arlington Robinson

Of no other contemporary American poet can it be said that religion was a major interest, unless one regards that word in its broadest significance and includes in it indirect expression. It is a striking fact that America, which has been identified with popular and even fundamental religion, has had few poets who have given expression to religious faith. I am not thinking now of Longfellow, Lowell, Holmes, Whittier, Lanier, and others who are discussed in chapter 13. It is a fact that there is no material in the major writers of the earlier period bearing upon our survey. In the poetry of Emerson, Whitman, and Poe one would never know that Jesus had lived. Emerson wrote a noteworthy passage on Jesus in his *Divinity Address,* but there is nothing about Jesus in his poetry. When we consider contemporary poets, we have to say that the same statement may be made of Robert Frost, Robinson Jeffers, Amy Lowell, Edgar Lee Masters, and many others. It is only here and there that one finds a poem of the best quality which relates in any way to Jesus.

One explanation of the melancholy and even pessimism of Edwin Arlington Robinson is that he found in his age so little of the faith that had characterized a former generation. No one has more poignantly expressed the significance of Calvary than has he in his sonnet:

Friendless and faint, with martyred steps and slow,
Faint for the flesh, but for the spirit free,
Stung by the mob that came to see the show,
The Master toiled along to Calvary;
We jibed him, as he went, with houndish glee,
Till his dim eyes for us did overflow;
We cursed his vengeless hands thrice wretchedly,—
And this was nineteen hundred years ago.

But after nineteen hundred years the shame
Still clings, and we have not made good the loss
That outraged faith has entered in his name.
Ah, when shall come love's courage to be strong!
Tell me, O Lord—tell me, O Lord, how long
Are we to keep Christ writhing on the cross! [7]

His poem "Nicodemus" [8] is based on an interview between Nicodemus and Caiaphas just before the trial of Jesus. Nicodemus says:

. . . What the man is,
Not what he was to unawakened eyes,

[7] "Calvary." Used by permission Charles Scribner's Sons.
[8] Copyright 1932, Edwin Arlington Robinson. Used by permission The Macmillan Co., publishers.

Engages those who have acknowledged him
And are alive today. . . .

. . . .

. . . Because we move,
And breathe, and say a few complacent words
With tongues that are afraid to say our thoughts,
We think we are alive. But we are dead.

Caiaphas tries to get Nicodemus to persuade Jesus
to leave Jerusalem. He is evidently afraid of him and
of what the law may do to him, but Nicodemus answers:

> . . . Because you are afraid,
> Must you see nothing in the world but fear?
> There is no fear in this man, Caiaphas.
> He shuns a little while a coming death,
> Which he foresees, that you and I may live.
>
> . . . .
>
> He tells me of light coming for the world,
> And of men loving darkness more than light.
> He is the light; and we who love the dark
> Because our fathers were at home in it,
> Would hound him off alone into the hills
> And laugh to see that we were rid of him.
>
> . . . .
>
> Come with me,
> But once, to see and hear him. . . .

This man's dying will not be death.

> All he could see through tears that blinded him
> To Caiaphas, to himself, and to all men
> Save one, was one that he had left alone,
> Alone in a bare room, and not afraid.

5. Carl Sandburg

Carl Sandburg has used Jesus to hit at the evils of
the American church. In his long poem *The People,
Yes*, in which we have suggestions of every phase of
American life in the homely phrases and catchwords
of the street and the factory, there occurs this passage:

> When violence is hired
> and murder is paid for
> and tear gas, clubs, automatics
>
> .   .   .   .
>
> join in the hoarse mandate,
> "Get the hell out of here,"
> why then reserve a Sabbath
> and call it a holiness day
> for the mention of Jesus Christ
> and why drag in the old quote,
> "Thou shalt love thy neighbor as thyself"? [9]

His indignation reaches its climax as he thinks of a
popular evangelist, perhaps Billy Sunday. His poem
"To a Contemporary Bunkshooter" is at once a pro-
test against the church that harbors such a demagogue
and a powerful representation of the true spirit of
Jesus. The evangelist is a sensationalist and a clown,
squirting words, smashing chairs, shaking his fist, con-
demning men to hell. He wants laborers to forget their
oppression and think only of mansions in the skies;
six-dollar-a-week department store girls are to look at

[9] Used by permission Harcourt, Brace & Co., Inc.

Jesus on the cross, and they will be satisfied. He culti-
vates the bankers and lawyers, although they are the
same type of men that crucified Jesus. Jesus would not
stand for such.

> He never came near clean people or dirty people but
> they felt cleaner because he came along. . . .
> . . . .
> He threw out something fresh and beautiful from the
> skin of his body and the touch of his hands wherever
> he passed along.

Sandburg challenges the evangelist to show where he
is pouring out the blood of his life and closes by saying:

> I've been to this suburb of Jerusalem they call Golgotha,
> where they nailed Him, and I know if the story is
> straight it was real blood ran from His Hands and
> the nail-holes, and it was real blood spurted in
> red drops where the spear of the Roman soldier
> rammed in between the ribs of this Jesus of Nazareth.[10]

This poem suggests that the poems recently written
about Jesus are apt to take the turn of protest against
the established order. It is often said that in labor meet-
ings, while the Church is hissed, the name of Jesus
awakens applause. The workers feel, as Sarah Cleghorn
expresses it in "Comrade Jesus," that he is their com-
rade and ought to be given their card. Likewise, the
Jew appeals to his spirit as rising above racial hatred.

[10] From *Chicago Poems*. Used by permission Henry Holt & Co., pub-
lishers.

Those who favor peace at any price are apt to summon Jesus as one of their chief supporters.

6. Negro Poets

Some of the Negro poets find a basis for Christian faith in Jesus' spirit of brotherhood and love, notably Countee Cullen and James Weldon Johnson. The latter's poem "O Black and Unknown Bards" raises the question as to how their lips touched the sacred fire, how in their darkness they came to know "the power and beauty of the minstrel lyre." Recalling such songs as "Steal Away to Jesus," "Nobody Knows de Trouble I See," "Go Down, Moses," "Ain't Goin' to Study War No More," Johnson says:

> You sang far better than you knew; the songs
> That for your listeners' hungry hearts sufficed
> Still live,—but more than this to you belongs:
> *You sang a race from wood and stone to Christ.*[11]

And this recalls the conclusion of that moving composite of music and poetry, *Green Pastures*, when Gabriel asks the Lord not to blow the trumpet for the destruction of mankind. God himself is thinking, especially of the words of the prophet Hosea, who said that man through suffering would find his way to a suffering God. "Did he mean that even God must suffer?" And then comes the voice: "Oh! look at him! dey goin' to

[11] From *Saint Peter Relates an Incident.* Used by permission The Viking Press, Inc., publisher.

make him carry it up dat hill! Dey goin' to nail him to it! Hallelujah, King Jesus."

Countee Cullen once complained that the Negro had been made black and then bidden to sing. How could he? And yet he has written some of the best lyric poems in American contemporary literature. He puts himself in the place of Simon the Cyrenian, who carried the cross when Jesus fainted beneath it. He refused at first because he seemed to think that Jesus made the appeal to him because his skin was black. On second thought he realized that there was something about him that was different from other men.

> But He was dying for a dream,
>   And He was very weak,
> And in His eyes there shone a gleam
>   Men journey far to seek.
>
> It was Himself by pity bought;
>   I did for Christ alone
> What all of Rome could not have wrought
>   With bruise of lash or stone.[12]

In his longer poem "The Black Christ" he deals with the lynching of his brother, which awakens in him a feeling of horror and even hatred. The mother of the two, with her faith in Christ, urges patience, in view of the fact that Christ himself had suffered a tragic

---

[12] "Simon the Cyrenian Speaks" from *Color*. Copyright 1925, Harper & Brothers. Used by permission.

death. The poet sees the suffering of the Negro in the light of the world's greatest tragedy. Calvary in Palestine is re-enacted in the suffering of a race.

> Two brothers have I had on earth,
> One of spirit, one of sod;
> My mother suckled one at birth,
> One was the Son of God.

His only hope is that such a crime might lead the white race eventually to awake to the horror of it and that there might come a greater faith, a wiser groping for the light.

> But where had swayed that misery
> Now only was a flowering tree
> That would soon travail into fruit.
> . . . .
> Now have we seen beyond degree
> That love which has no boundary;
> Our eyes have looked on Calvary.[18]

A striking confirmation of the importance of this Negro poetry in modern American life is found in Arnold J. Toynbee's *Study of History*. Speaking of the difficulties under which various nations and races have worked out their civilizations, the obstacles they had to overcome, and especially the Negro's lot of slavery, he notices that the Negro did not bring any ancestral

---

[18] From *The Black Christ and Other Poems*. Copyright 1920, Harper & Brothers. Used by permission.

religion from Africa and that what few fragments there were, were quickly forgotten.

Thus he came to America spiritually as well as physically naked; and he has met the emergency by covering his nakedness with his enslaver's cast-off clothes. The Negro has adapted himself to his new social environment by rediscovering in Christianity certain original meanings and values which Western Christendom has long ignored. Opening a simple and impressionable mind to the Gospels, he has discovered that Jesus was a prophet who came into the world not to confirm the mighty in their seats but to exalt the humble and meek.

Comparing them to the early Christians who brought Christianity to Rome and "thereby performed the miracle of establishing a new religion which was alive in the place of an old religion which was already dead," Toynbee says it is possible that the Negro immigrants who have found Christianity in America may perform the greater miracle of raising the dead to life.

With childlike spiritual intuition and their genius for giving spontaneous esthetic expression to emotional religious experience, they may perhaps be capable of kindling the cold grey ashes of Christianity which have been transmitted to them by us until, in their hearts, the divine fire glows again. It is thus perhaps . . . that Christianity may conceivably become the living faith of a dying civilization for the second time.[14]

[14] P. 129. Used by permission Oxford University Press, New York.

CHAPTER XVII

The Future of Faith

IN THE poets and poems of our own day I have tried to
suggest various points of view and various kinds of
verse. It is clearly impossible to discuss in detail many
others that are just as interesting and important.[1] One
is overwhelmed with the amount of poetry that has been
published in this country and England since the be-
ginning of the century. Each decade has furnished a
new group of poets, who have been heralded in separate
volumes, in anthologies, in poetry magazines of every
description. No subject is more popular in colleges and
universities or in women's clubs. The poets themselves
have by readings and lectures increased the interest of
the general public. Literary factions have followed
each other: Frost and Robinson, Eliot and Pound,

[1] Some poems about Christ not mentioned in the text are: Lola
Ridge, "Firehead"; W. B. Yeats, "The Resurrection"; James Branch
Cabell, "Easter Eve"; Leonora Speyer, "Oberammergau"; Lizette W.
Reese, "A Carol and a Christmas Folk Song"; Sara Teasdale, "In the
Carpenter Shop"; W. W. Gibson, "The Conscript"; Alice Meynell,
"Thou Art the Way"; Oscar Wilde, "E Tenebris"; Joyce Kilmer, Col-
lected Poems; William Vaughn Moody, "Good Friday Night"; George
Santayana, "O Martyred Spirit"; Elinor Wylie, "Peter and John";
Eunice Tietjens, "The Great Man"; Henry van Dyke, "A Lost Word
of Jesus"; Gilbert Chesterton, "The Donkey"; Dorothy Parker, "The
Maid-Servant at the Inn," "Prayer for a New Mother"; W. A. Percy,
"His Peace"; Edwin Markham, "The Nail-torn God." See also the
references to contemporary poets in ch. i.

were succeeded by Auden and Spender and Lewis, and they in turn by Patchen, Fearing, and the apocalypse group in England, and more recently by Delmore Schwartz, Karl Shapiro, and Robert Lowell. And the end is not yet.

In this survey we are not concerned with many aspects of contemporary poetry but only with their bearing on the central theme of this volume. There are many conservatives who will have nothing to do with poetry written after Tennyson or Kipling. The general impression is that the later poetry is obscure and that it is nearly always opposed to the tradition of English verse. Still others object that it reveals only the seamy side of life, as do modern fiction and modern drama. They will have none of it. The conservative does not realize that the same objection has been raised in every new age of poetry. Shakespeare was said to have violated the classic unities; Donne and Blake were as eccentric in their verse as they were obscure in their thought. To go no farther back than Browning and Whitman, we know that they had to wait a generation to be recognized as major poets—Browning from the standpoint of obscurity and Whitman from that of obscenity and revolutionary technique. As to the charge of obscurity, this needs to be said: all great poems demand concentration and rereading. There are some that demand not only close attention but patience and effort, and even interpretation. Donne, Eliot, and Hopkins are good illustrations of poets who write this type of poetry, but the results justify all the labor given. There are other poets whom no special pleading can absolve from what seems like willful obscurity. Unless one had a lifetime to work out such puzzles, the reading would be futile; and frequently when the poets themselves or their admirers have found the interpretation, there is little of value. Much of it is mere nonsense written for coteries and disciples.

So much for the conservative reaction to modern poetry. The radicals have contended that new experiences born out of individual lives and out of the complex civilization of this age have all affected men's minds and morals. It would be a miracle if poetry had not been affected by modern psychology and other sciences, by the greed of industrialism and the signs of a machine age, and above all by two world wars. New experiences of thought and feeling necessarily lead to experiments in the technique of verse. W. H. Auden, in his "Letter to Lord Byron," characterizes his compeers in poetry.

> Many are in tears;
> Some have returned to bed and locked the doors;
> And some swing mostly from the chandeliers;
> Some have passed out entirely in the rears;
> Some have been sick in corners; the sobering few
> Are trying hard to think of something new.[2]

---

[2] Used by permission Random House, Inc.

The last line is a good characterization of experimentalists like E. E. Cummings, Oscar Williams, and Wallace Stevens.

C. Day Lewis in his *Hope for Poetry* uses the parable of the prodigal son to illustrate what he considers the value of the experiments in technique and content in contemporary poetry.

The younger son, fretting against parental authority, weary of sentimentalism, suspecting that the soul needs a rest, has packed his bag and set out for a far country. Rumors of his doings come to our ears; they are generally unfavorable and always distorted, for they have had to pass across seas. He is flirting with foreign whores or with ghosts; he has wasted his fortune; he has forgotten how to speak English; he has shamed his father; he has gone much in the desert. Only his father smiles indulgently with secret pride, amused at the vigor of his seed. Then the younger son returns, not a broken prodigal, but healthy, wealthy and wise. He has many acres under cultivation over there; he has money in the bank, strange tales to tell us, and some fine children already.

Thus in parable form one of the leading contemporary poets suggests what may have come out of the experiences of the poets and out of their experiments with all forms of verse technique. It creates in one who has been accustomed to the traditional view of poetry a certain intellectual curiosity to explore what has happened during the past generation.

The question as to what valuable things the prodigal sons of modern verse have brought back from their wanderings in strange lands is perhaps best answered by Karl Shapiro in his *Essay on Rime,* written in poetic form. It is all the more important because it was written from the perspective of the Far East while he was in the Second World War, during which he found some time to review the main movements in modern poetry. The poem is divided into three parts under the general theme of confusion—confusion in prosody, in language, and in belief. It is only the latter with which we are now concerned. Although disclaiming the dialectic as having anything to do with poetry, he analyzes the points of view from which poets write. He begins with Hart Crane, whose death was an "act of shame, bewilderment and contrition." He is the tragic figure who suffered from maladjustment in his age; "apart from love, apart from hate, apart from sure belief," he "leaped from the deck-rail of his disbelief to senseless strangulation." Many have followed in the wake of his confusion. Shapiro speaks of the "intellectuals," who "bay like demons at us"; the history of the failure in belief is an "encyclopedic inquiry." Eliot alone, by naming faith a positive attribute, "has justified his interest in belief," and yet few would follow him in his retreat to the Anglican faith. The "amoralists" regard piety as an outlandish manifestation of genius. Those who have followed modern science have often regarded man as beast and beast as man. The Age of

Reason walked beside the Age of Progress toward the Age of War. The Marxist poets, while rightly drawing their indictment against the modern social order, laid too much stress on the "economic absolute" and tended to rob man of deity. The followers of Freud have considered art a branch of clinical analysis and adopted the symbolism of laboratories and clinics, and unveiled "the dark psyche which governs us." There are various substitute beliefs growing out of personal predilections, but none are valid; fantasy mixes with them, as in the case of Yeats, who in his later years found satisfaction in a "toy universe with gyres and spooky fires and even table rapping." The criticism that has sought to interpret these various beliefs is characterized by horror for emotions or fear of beauty; such a cleavage there never was before between audience and poet and critic. The conclusion of the whole matter is that contemporary poetry leads to the "dead hand and exhaustion of our rime," and that the only aftermath of poetry should be love.

Now our question is, What is to be gained from this confusion of beliefs or lack of belief? It will not do to wave all this aside. There is truth in Mary Colum's statement that we are witnessing the ruins of a world, but we must study the ruins. Dante could hardly have written his *Purgatory* and *Paradise* if he had not passed through the circles of *Hell*. The very cynicism and pessimism of many modern poets may be an incentive to faith. When Ezra Pound speaks of a "botched civilization," symbolized by "an old bitch gone in the teeth"; when T. S. Eliot writes his early poems with the background of the desert through which we are passing; when Conrad Aiken speaks of the "strewn wreck of the World," "sadness unplumbed; misery without bound"; when Louis MacNeice bases a poem on a conversation between a city man and a country man in England, with each of them expressing in vivid words the failure of his environment—"endless liabilities, no assets"—and then ironically suggests that it is Christmas morn; when E. E. Cummings addresses "King Christ" and suggests that "this world is all aleak" and "life preservers there are none"—then it is time for men of faith to see the significance of modern perdition.

As Amos N. Wilder in his book *The Spiritual Aspects of the New Poetry* well says, it is the asceticism of Jesus that drives many modern poets away from him.

The very medium of their art as poets, indeed the very element of their experience as men, is the gamut of human living, emotion, drama. "Man's resinous heart" and the loves, loyalties, the pride, the grief it feeds—these are the stuff of poetry and the sense of life. And the Cross lays its shadow on this; it draws away all the blood from the glowing body of existence and leaves it mutilated and charred in the hope of some thin ethereal felicity. The wine of life is changed to water. The spectrum, incredibly enough, is surrendered for an undifferentiated and commonplace white light. The "dramatic caves" of the human heart and imagination are renounced for some wan empryean of spiritual reverie. The very word "spiritual" has come to signify inanity and vacuity. The refusal of religion by the modern poets, and by more than modern and by more than poets, goes back to the apparent denial of human living by religion, to the supposed incompatibility of Life with life and art with faith.[3]

This, as we have already seen, is the reason Yeats rejected Christianity and seemed to put the worship of Dionysus or Plotinus in its place, and many other poets have consciously or unconsciously followed in his wake. They seem to know nothing of the abundant life, which includes all knowledge and all the arts and all the culture of the world, as the distinctive interpretation of contemporary liberal preachers; they know nothing of the secret and the method of Jesus as interpreted by Arnold or the fullness of his personality as interpreted by Browning.

And yet when all has been said about the neglect of Jesus in modern poetry, one finds many surprises, like those already suggested. Marianne Moore, one of the chief experimentalists in verse and one of the most modern of the moderns, in her poem "In Distrust of Merits" refers to the star of David, the star of Bethlehem, the "black imperial lion of the Lord," as the emblem of a risen world.

Wallace Stevens, in one of his best poems, "Sunday Morning"—a sketch of a woman who is the counterpart of Eliot's Prufrock—speaks of the "dark encroachment

[3] Used by permission the publisher, Harper & Brothers.

of that old catastrophe [the crucifixion]" breaking upon the complacency of her conventional faith as she thinks for a moment of Palestine, "dominion of the blood and sepulchre." Edith Sitwell, the most sophisticated of the sophisticates, writing of the raids on England in 1940, finds a parallel in the blood of Christ, "the Starved Man hung upon the Cross."

Robinson Jeffers, who generally appears not as an ineffectual angel beating his luminous wings in the void but as an evil spirit beating his wings in the dark, wrote *Dear Judas*, in which he represents Jesus as saying:

> ... What's kingdom to *me?*
> To me that walked with God my Father before the
>   foundation of the earth? I ruled the angels in heaven:
> And now I have come to a little place to save a lost
>   people.

And again:

> ... I am making a new thing in the world,
> I am making a kingdom not built on blood, I am mak-
>   ing a power weaponed with love not violence.[4]

In a totally unexpected tender poem addressed to his father he writes:

> Christ was your lord and captain all your life,
> He fails the world, but you he did not fail,

[4] Used by permission Random House, Inc.

He led you through all forms of grief and strife,
Intact, a man full armed.[5]

D. H. Lawrence, who sought to take us back into primitive ways, in one of his lucid intervals spoke of Christianity as the greatest thing in the history of the world, but added that it had had its day and must be considered one of the has-beens. Robert Graves recently wrote a novel entitled *King Jesus,* which is based upon the fantastic idea that Jesus was the son of a Caesar; but Graves has one of his leading characters say:

What an extraordinary story it is, too! Slave to books though I am, I have never in all my reading come across its match. . . . To be laid at birth in a manger-basket, to be crowned king, to suffer voluntarily on a cross, to conquer death, to become immortal: such was the destiny of this last and noblest scion of the most venerable royal line in the world.

And one who heard Jesus only once, when he blessed the children, says: "My world at that time was lit by a soft inexplicable radiance, which gave a sheen to the commonest objects on which it shone."

What do these scattered quotations from some of the most typical and radical contemporary poets signify? And what about the faith in Jesus that we have found in Eliot, Masefield, and Lindsay? Perhaps they foreshadow some order that may come out of the chaos of

[5] Used by permission Random House, Inc.

modern thought. Patrick Kirby, one of the minor poets of this era, wrote:

> Only out of chaos
> Creation;
> Only out of confusion
> Order;
> Only from our decay,
> The new shoots of a New Earth;
> Only out of our darkness
> Light unquenchable,
> And a new Heaven
> Filled with new stars! [6]

Such an outcome from the complex and dark period through which we are passing might be realized if more and more poets would, like Eliot, return to the poets who represent a great tradition—to Dante, Donne, Milton, Blake, Browning. They also might find some light thrown on the modern search for truth by philosophers, historians, scientists, and great humanists. If, as we have found, poets are especially sensitive to the intellectual currents of their age, they may find that the way has been prepared by men in other fields for a new age of faith. Maxwell Anderson in his preface to the play *Journey to Jerusalem* tells of how he came to accept Christianity as the surest bulwark against despair. He went back to a study of the origin of Christianity and found the teachings of Jesus "the most con-

---

[6] "Song for These Days" from *Poet on Mule* (copyright 1940, Patrick F. Kirby). Used by permission the author.

vincing evidence of what we are accustomed to call inspiration."

The words of the Sermon on the Mount seem to cut across the dark sky of Palestine under the Caesars like God's own levin flash, lighting up centuries past and centuries to come. . . . I know of no other poem, book, play, passage or sermon which compresses so much dynamic and shattering wisdom into words. . . . He came at a time much like our own in many ways, only further gone into the abyss of despair and surrender. I wanted modern men and women, sitting in an audience, to grasp the problem of unfaith as it presented itself to Jesus. . . . This story of the Child of God in the court of the Sanhedrin, finding His way to the meaning of the universe as He walks alone among the columns—this appeared to me the perfect symbol of the soul of man searching for its own meaning.[7]

It is a commonplace to say that modern science has made faith seem impossible to contemporary leaders. It should be known by now that scientists like Einstein, Eddington, Millikan, and Compton have demolished the idea of a material universe dominated by chance and interpreted only by the philosophy of determinism. In his recently published volume *Human Destiny* Lecomte du Noüy has profited by the scientific research of such men and has gone even further in a Christian interpretation of scientific facts. He does not stop with the emphasis upon spiritual or religious values; he goes the whole way in interpreting such values in the light

[7] Used by permission Anderson House.

of the Christian revelation. He makes it clear that intelligence alone cannot solve individual or world problems. He finds in evolution the basis for a profound belief in the possible future of mankind, in which growth will take place in the realm of the moral and spiritual and will develop the idea of human dignity. "Men must be made to understand that the important thing is to develop what is within them, to purify themselves, to better themselves, *to come closer to the perfect ideal which is Christ.*" Men will work against evolution if intelligence alone rules and not the sense of duty, of liberty, of dignity, of the beauty of disinterested effort. Man may become a co-worker with God.

He needs enlightenment, encouragement, advice, consolation and hope. Efficient, disinterested help can only come to him from the wise, inspired human tradition represented by the Christian religion, heir to all the spiritual treasures of mankind and keeper of the eternal flame which the greatest and purest men have passed on to one another, from time immemorial, over the bodies of dying civilizations.

The philosophers have their answer too. Santayana in some of his books has seemed to be a skeptic, a rationalist, at times a naturalist; but mankind may remember his sonnet on faith longer than some of his philosophical works. He recently has made a profound study of the idea of Christ—God in man—as found in the Gospels and especially the Fourth Gospel. While he does not accept wholeheartedly the theology he interprets, he shows that it is central in his thinking. Much earlier he wrote a volume entitled *Poetry and Religion*, in which he spoke of the identical origins of both. Dante showed in a supreme way this union of dogma and poetry—his poem is "a picture of human destiny, an epic containing the moral autobiography of man. . . . What is false in the science of facts may be true in the science of values." Santayana then raises the question as to whether Christianity can stand. The greatest calamity would be that no other religion would take its place.

The European races would then be reduced to confessing that while they had mastered the mechanical forces in nature, both by science and arts, they had become incapable of mastering or understanding themselves . . . and could find no way of uttering the ideal meaning of their life.

He suggests accordingly that the idea of Christ promises something spiritual, something greater, and that if he were accepted, the world might have a new era of faith.

In Arnold J. Toynbee's monumental *Study of History* the amount of space given to various aspects of the part played by Jesus and Christianity in the history of the world is in sharp contrast with Wells's *Outline of History* and many other historical works. Even in the one-volume condensation there is much space given to Jesus, especially in the presentation of the various kinds of saviors the world has followed—the savior with the sword, the savior who has led men either to the past or to a Utopian future, the philosopher-king type envisaged by Plato, and the savior who is God incarnate in a man. There have been many instances of the last type, but Toynbee distinguishes sharply between Jesus, Hercules, Orpheus, and others about whom legends arose.

When we set out on this quest we found ourselves moving in the midst of a mighty host, but, as we have pressed forward, the marchers, company by company, have fallen out of the race. The first to fail were the swordsmen, the next the archaists and futurists, the next the philosophers, until only gods were left in the running. At the final ordeal of death, few, even of these would-be saviour gods, have dared to put their title to the test by plunging into the icy river. And now as we stand and gaze with our eyes fixed upon the farther shore, a single figure rises from the flood and straightway fills the whole horizon. There is the Saviour; "and the pleasure of the Lord shall prosper in his hand; he shall see of the travail of his soul and shall be satisfied." [8]

In comparing Jesus with others from the standpoint of detachment from the world and from that of transfiguration, Toynbee reaches a climax in the idea that Christ, while detached from the world, is a part of it; that while he reached certain divine moments in his

[8] P. 547. Used by permission Oxford University Press, New York.

life, he looks forward to the establishment of the kingdom of God in this world.

If we ask how, in fact, God's will can be done on Earth as it is in Heaven, the answer, given in the technical language of theology, is that the omnipresence of God involves His immanence in This World and in every living soul in it, as well as His transcendent existence on supra-mundane planes. In the Christian conception of the Godhead His transcendent aspect (or 'person') is displayed in God the Father and His immanent aspect in God the Holy Ghost; but the distinctive and crucial feature of the Christian Faith is that God is not a Duality but a Trinity in Unity, and that in His aspect as God the Son the other two aspects are unified in a Person who, in virtue of this mystery, is as accessible to the human heart as is He incomprehensible to the human understanding. In the Person of Christ Jesus—Very God yet also Very Man—the divine society and the mundane society have a common member who in This World is born into the ranks of the proletariat and dies the death of a malefactor, while in the Other World He is the King of God's Kingdom, a King who is God Himself.[9]

Where can there be found a better statement of the Incarnation than in these words of a great historian and social scientist:

The divine nature, in so far as it is accessible to us, must have something in common with our own; and, if we look for one particular spiritual faculty which we are conscious of possessing and which we also can attribute

[9] *Ibid.*, pp. 529-30.

with absolute confidence to God—because God would be spiritually inferior to man . . . if this faculty were not in Him but were nevertheless in us—then the faculty which we shall think of first as being common to man and God will be one which the philosophers wish to mortify; and that is the faculty of Love.[10]

It is well known that Whitehead, whom many consider the foremost philosopher in the English-speaking world, has in his *Science and the Modern World* and *Religion in the Making* expounded the limitations of science and the need for poetry and religion. While he laments the fact that both Christianity and Buddhism have lost their ancient hold upon the world, he still contends in his *Adventure in Ideas* that Christianity "endowed mankind with its most precious instrument of progress—the impracticable ethics of Christ." He emphasizes the importance of great historical occasions in which humanity reaches its highest points, and especially the life and teachings of Jesus. "The essence of Christianity is the appeal to the life of Christ, as a revelation of the nature of God and of his agency in the world." And he continues, "The Mother, the Child, and the bare manger, the lowly man, homeless and self-forgetful, with his message of peace, love, and sympathy; the suffering, the agony, the tender words as life ebbed, the final despair; and the whole with the authority of supreme victory"—these are unique from the standpoint of both philosophy and history.

[10] *Ibid.*, p. 530.

He contends that the power of Christianity lies in its "revelation in act of that which Plato defined in theory." Origen, Augustine, and a few others have the distinction of being the only thinkers in fundamental metaphysical doctrine who have improved on Plato. "The world for Plato includes only the image of God, an imitation of his ideas, and never God and his idea." Here alone we have the direct immanence of God in the person of Christ and one of those profound flashes of insight that illuminate the world. Christianity represents the two unfailing visions of life—the dream of youth and the harvest of tragedy—and it furnishes that peace which passes all understanding, "that Harmony of Harmonies which calms destructive turbulence and completes civilization."

To somewhat the same conclusion came Paul Elmer More, who in his later years turned his attention more and more to the study of philosophy and religion. Long regarded as perhaps the best-equipped literary critic in America by reason of his knowledge of ancient and modern languages and literature, he undertook a study of the relation of Plato's philosophy to Christian literature and tradition, thus breaking sharply with his colleague in humanism, Irving Babbitt, in maintaining that true humanism could not leave out the consideration of religion as a paramount influence in life and thought. There is every evidence that he began with the conviction that the Platonic philosophy was the basis of what was best in Christianity, but his volume entitled

Christ: The Word is a profound statement of the value and authority of the Incarnation as the fulfillment of all that was best in Plato's ideas. If one does not care to assess the relative importance of the two systems of thought, he can at least agree with More that "the two traditions together constitute the greatest effort of the human mind to find at once an ultimate religion and philosophy." Plato's *Dialogues,* so well interpreted in a previous volume by More, fall bodily into the Christian scheme. Plato was dimly aware of a theophany to come, of which his allegories were a prophecy. Socrates in the *Apology* told his friends that the full truth could not be known until revealed to man by the grace of God. Plato would have thought that Christianity gave precisely the one thing for which he had been searching all his life. If he had heard Jesus talk of the Father, he would doubtless, according to More, have exclaimed, "My Lord and my God!"

Christianity, More thought, was therefore not only the fulfillment of Hebrew prophecy but the consummation of Greek philosophy. In the Fourth Gospel "the fine flower of Platonism blossomed after long centuries in a strange garden."

The Word of God, as Wisdom itself, as Beauty itself, and Holiness, has shown itself embodied in a human character. The Christian philosophy develops and clarifies and vivifies the Platonic tradition. It acquires a dynamic hold on the imagination and will which as pure philosophy it could not possess.

No finer statement has ever been made of the doctrine of the Logos than that found in chapters 10 and 11 of More's volume:

The Logos is the shaping and governing intelligence in the universe . . . a divine *purpose* realizing itself through the ages—"the manifold wisdom of God, according to the eternal purpose (*prothesis*) which He purposed in Christ Jesus." . . . Evil through man's freedom came to thwart this purpose. The world knew him not. What was to be done? As the Logos was the instrument of creation, it should be the instrument of restoration. There was needed a more direct illumination than is afforded by the logical order of nature and life. At the climax of the drama the Logos comes forth upon the stage and takes its part. If there be a God, is it not reasonable that He should reveal himself as one who should be imitated, who should bestow grace upon his followers, and as the spirit who should guide them into all truth? By the dogma of vicarious atonement the pains and losses and failures of our mortal state become part of a cosmic agony, and any feeling of resentment at the real or seeming injustices of life fades away into awe before the spectacle of the Cross.[11]

The conclusion is inevitable from this brief survey of some of the most important modern thinkers: The poets have failed to understand some of the main currents of modern thought. They have not been wise leaders. There is no one poet who stands out as did some of the poets of previous periods. Only now and then in flashes of insight do we have a suggestion of a better

[11] Used by permission Princeton University Press.

future. Yeats expressed the hope of an age of faith:

> O silver trumpets, be ye lifted up,
> And cry to the great race that is to come!
> . . . .
> That race may hear our music and awake.[12]

And Stephen Spender has expressed in memorable words a possible world that may emerge from the chaos of the present age.

> Oh comrades, let not those who follow after
> —The beautiful generation that shall spring from our sides—
> Let not them wonder how after the failure of banks
> The failure of cathedrals and the declared insanity of our
>   rulers,
> We lacked the Spring-like resources of the tiger
> Or of plants who strike out new roots to gushing waters.
> But through torn-down portions of old fabric let their eyes
> Watch the admiring dawn explode like a shell
> Around us, dazing us with its light like snow.[13]

[12] From *Collected Poems* (copyright 1933, The Macmillan Co.). Used by permission the publishers.

[13] From "After They Have Tired." Used by permission Random House, Inc.

Suggestions for Further Reading

GENERAL BOOKS

Cecil, Lord David. *The Oxford Book of Christian Verse.*
Hill, Caroline M. *The World's Great Religious Poetry.*
Noyes, Alfred. *The Golden Book of Catholic Verse.*
Osgood, Charles G. *Poetry as a Means of Grace.*
Wagenknecht, Edward. *The Story of Jesus in the World's Literature.*

THE POETS OF THE SEVENTEENTH CENTURY

Dowden, Edward. *Puritan and Anglican.*
Gosse, Edmund. *Life and Letters of John Donne.*
————. *Seventeenth Century Studies.*
Grierson, H. J. C. *Cross Currents in English Literature of the Seventeenth Century.*
————. *Metaphysical Lyrics and Poems of the Seventeenth Century.*
Heyward, John, ed. *Complete Poems and Selected Prose of John Donne.* Nonesuch Press.
Martin, L. C., ed. *Poetical Works of Richard Crashaw.*
————. *Works of Henry Vaughan.*
Palmer, G. H., ed. *The English Works of George Herbert.*
Wade, Gladys I., ed. *Poetical Works of Thomas Traherne.*
Walton, Izaak. *Lives* (Donne and Herbert).
White, Helen C. *The Metaphysical Poets.*

WILLIAM BLAKE

Gardner, Charles. *Vision and Vesture.*
Kazin, Alfred, ed. *The Portable Blake.*
Keynes, Geoffrey, ed. *Complete Writings.* Nonesuch Press.
Schorer, Mark. *The Politics of Vision.*

Standard one-volume editions of Milton, Arnold, Tennyson, Browning, Holmes, Whittier, Longfellow, Lowell, Bryant, and Lanier.

CONTEMPORARY POETRY

Drew, Elizabeth, and Sweeney, John L. *Directions in Modern Poetry.*

Eliot, T. S. *Collected Poems.*

Gregory, Horace. *The Triumph of Life.*

Gregory, Horace, and Zaturenska, Marya. *History of American Poetry, 1900-1940.*

Hopkins, Gerard Manley. *Poems* (notes by Robert Bridges).

Luccock, Halford. *Contemporary American Literature and Religion.*

——, ed. *The Questing Spirit.*

Matthiessen, F. O. *The Achievement of T. S. Eliot.*

Meynell, Everard. *Life of Francis Thompson.*

Thompson, Francis. *Complete Poetical Works.*

Untermeyer, Louis. *Modern American Poetry and Modern English Poetry.* One-volume ed.

Williams, Oscar. *A Little Treasury of Modern Poetry.*

Index